MARK GRUNER'S NUMBERS OF LIFE

MARK GRUNER'S NUMBERS OF LIFE

An Introduction to Numerology

MARK GRUNER and CHRISTOPHER K. BROWN

Taplinger Publishing Company | New York

First American Edition Published in 1978 by
TAPLINGER PUBLISHING CO., INC.
New York, New York

Library of Congress Cataloging in Publication Data

Gruner, Mark.
Mark Gruner's Numbers of life.

First published under title: Numbers of life.
1. Symbolism of numbers.   I. Brown, Christopher K., joint author.
II. Title.   III. Title: Numbers of life.
BF1623.P9G77   1978   133.3′35   78–57560

ISBN 0–8008–5639–2 (Cloth)   ISBN 0–8008–5640–9 (Paper)

Book design: Mollie M. Torras

It is traditional these days to dedicate a book to one
or more individuals who have helped and encouraged or even
motivated the author to put pen to paper.

We, however, are in the unique position to be able
to dedicate this book to some sixty thousand people,
of every nationality, who have provided the facts and
experience to make this book possible. So to these people,
wherever they may be—thank you. But there are a few
special people we must mention for their consideration,
assistance, and everlasting encouragement.

To John Sleeman, Suzanne Lucas, Gary Shaw,
Anne Lawson, Edmund Layton, Georgina and Frank Baychek
we would like to say thank you.

But above all to Robyn, Margaret, George, Stella,
Reneé, and Karen, for without their love and understanding
this book would not have been possible.

Contents

Foreword

Has a particular number proved to be significant in your life, occurring time and time again? Your answer will probably be yes, as most of us seem to attract one number that occurs with above average regularity throughout our lives.

This book is about that number—your number. Hence the title *Numbers of Life*. Whether you like it or not your life is indeed ruled by numbers, for without them, life as we now know it would cease to function.

If numbers are significant within your life, you at least owe it to yourself to explore the mysteries of this phenomenon, if only to satisfy your curiosity.

Better still, let's explore the ancient art of numbers together—for hand in hand we will transport the mysteries of the past into our lives of the present. We will not only dissect our innermost desires, strong points, weak points, and character traits through this science, but we will learn how to do likewise for our friends, families, and associates. We will endeavor to reveal our true purpose in life and then we will set the wheels of success into motion.

Together, we will find how rhythm affects our very being and how we can tune into the rhythm of the universe to attract what is rightfully ours. We will learn how to organize ourselves and our day-to-day life to obtain contentment and peace of mind. We will use the rules and laws of life to recreate the very being that we would like to be. We will do this and more together, for as we share our newfound knowledge, we create awareness and spiritual understanding. Let's learn, understand, practice, and, above all, live the life we were really meant to—as a totally complete individual.

Numbers of life is about you and me.

Within These Pages Lie the Answers
to Many of Life's Problems

Your Personal Natal Chart

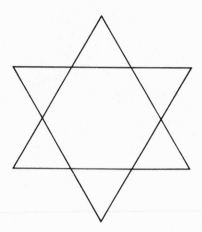

Name ————————————————————————————

Date of Birth: Month ☐   Day ☐   Year ☐

  Life Path Number = ☐

Information relating to the compilation of your own natal Numerological chart will be found in Chapters 4 through 10.

All the calculations in this book follow the American style of putting the number for the month first and then the number for the day.

1

A World Without Numbers

As you sit reading this book, look around you. What do you see? A table, chairs, curtains, carpets, television, radio. Now try to find one thing within this area that could be conceived without the power of numbers. Try as you may, you will be unable to find any item around you that has not relied on the law of numbers. Your home could not have been designed or even built without numbers. The same applies to your table, chairs, curtains, carpets, television, and radio—for without numbers, life as we now know it cannot function.

As an interesting exercise, try to live one day of your life without using numbers. Remember you cannot look at your watch, set the dial on the radio, use the telephone, write a letter, drive your car, catch the right bus, ride a bicycle, or even eat. Numbers obviously apply to all material objects, but do numbers apply to anything else? Let's look at some less tangible examples to see if the same law applies. You could not play or learn a musical instrument without the use of numbers, for without numbers there would be no music. Your children could not be educated without numbers, for education is based on numbers. You could not be treated in the hospital for diseases or ailments, without numbers, for the medical profession relies heavily on them. We judge an individual's maturity by his or her age and his or her level of affluence by numbers. You could not vote, governments could not govern, and wars could not happen—such is the power of numbers.

It is pointless to spend valuable time or space giving the complete history of numbers and Numerology, because we, the authors, firmly believe that Numerology is a now subject. You cannot change the past but you can shape the future. However, to satisfy the history lovers among us, we will devote just a few lines to some important historical stepping-stones that have made Numerology the thought-provoking subject it is today.

Great minds think alike and this is why numbers cannot be effectively traced back to any one given time or civilization. Philosophers from different civilizations and races were developing their own method of the written number. The Egyptians, Chinese, Hebrews, Indians, Sumerians, Chaldeans, and Phoenicians were all responsible for the furtherment of numbers. However, it was not until the sixth century B.C. that Pythagoras brought about the turning point in the history of Numerology. It is worth noting that the concepts of Numerology have been studied and upheld by some of the world's greatest philosophers and mathematicians. Brilliant men, who not only used their genius to discover or create momentous concepts that are still used today, but men who with their far-reaching mental capacity endorsed and built upon the basic philosophies of numbers.

Pythagoras was not only a brilliant mathematician, but a profound philosopher. He believed that the universe existed on numbers and that nothing could exist without numbers. Mathematicians are renowned for being logical people, for it is this power of logic that mathematics is based upon. Pythagoras used his profound logic to take mathematics one step further and deduce that if numbers provided the basis of the universe, then numbers must also provide the basis for life. Thus, the principles of Numerology were conceived. It is rewarding to note that this ever-changing, fast-moving civilization we now live in is rapidly returning to the ancient philosophies and wisdoms of the past, rediscovering with renewed vigor the life-styles and beliefs of those who lived many thousands of years before.

So, as you progress through this book, remember you are unfolding the pages of time and learning a subject that has been used by many brilliant mathematicians and philosophers. It is indeed an honor to follow in the footsteps of these individuals. So respect your task and use the new knowledge that you gain for the advancement of yourself and mankind.

2

The Most Important Event

Numerology separates all individuals into twelve basic types, depending on their life path number. This life path number is also referred to as the destiny or birth number, but by whatever title it is recognized, the meaning remains the same.

The most important event throughout man's life is the date on which he was born. He enters the world on a specific day of a month of a year. Everything in life has a purpose, a purpose that may usually seem clear and understandable, but can sometimes be surrounded by Providence. As children, our cycle of life and purpose commences. We attend school each day so that we may gain knowledge. We use this knowledge in later years to earn rewards for our effort. This material gain is in turn used to feed and clothe ourselves. As each day progresses we gain under-standing, awareness, and experience of life so that we may impart this knowledge to others. We marry, conceive, and raise children, following the same pattern that our parents followed. Such is the never-ending cycle of life, that *should the infinite purpose be removed, life itself would cease to exist.*

Nature has not created a haphazard existence that changes from generation to generation. It conforms to standardization. Why? Simply because purpose can only be founded on an organized existence. No man can say that conception, confinement, and birth are nonpurposeful events. *We cannot defy the law of purpose.* We were placed on this earth by a purpose, for a purpose, and to end with a purpose. Therefore our date of birth is all important, as it heralds our individual purpose in life, a purpose that might be totally or partly fulfilled. As life is purpose, the individual is also purpose, thus creating the basis of Numerology.

You will learn in the next chapter how to take the individual digits from a date of birth and compile a natal Numerological chart. This chart represents the total individual person and defines him or her accordingly, with a great deal of accuracy. However, before we can proceed to analyze any individual, we must learn how to calculate his or her life path number. It is worth mentioning here that unlike many other Numerologists we disagree with the basic teaching that the life path number is all important to the natal chart. Our experience has shown conclusively that true accuracy can only be gained from the natal chart analysis. However, we do agree that the life path number is important but that it should only be used to complement the natal chart.

Calculation of Life Path Number

It is a simple exercise to calculate any individual's life path number. Practice will enable you to complete this exercise in seconds. However, we strongly advise that initially you adhere to the following steps:

To find the life path number for an individual born on December 6, 1943:

Step a. Reduce the full birth date to numbers:
12/6/1943

Step b. Add all the digits of the birth date together *individually*:
$1 + 2 + 6 + 1 + 9 + 4 + 3 = 26$

Step c. Add the remaining two digits together:
$2 + 6 = 8$

The life path number for an individual born on December 6, 1943, is 8.

There are two further points to remember:
1. Do not count zero as a number.
2. Do not reduce the birth number addition, if the remaining numbers are 11, 22, and 33, as these are the master numbers of Numerology.

Throughout this book, examples have been used to illustrate the various calculations. Experience has shown this to be the easiest and most effective way to teach Numerology. So let us look at nine more examples to illustrate all the possible combinations and deviations that can occur.

Example 1
   To calculate the life path number for an individual born on May 15, 1960:

   Step a. Reduce the full birth date to numbers:
   5/15/1960
   Step b. Add all the digits of the birth date together *individually*:
   $5 + 1 + 5 + 1 + 9 + 6 + 0 = 27$
   Step c. Add the remaining two digits together:
   $2 + 7 = 9$
The life path number for an individual born on May 15, 1960, is 9.

Example 2
   To calculate the life path number for an individual born on November 29, 1948:

   Step a. Reduce the full birth date to numbers:
   11/29/1948
   Step b. Add all the digits of the birth date together *individually*:
   $1 + 1 + 2 + 9 + 1 + 9 + 4 + 8 = 35$
   Step c. Add the remaining two digits together:
   $3 + 5 = 8$
The life path number for an individual born on November 29, 1948, is 8.

Example 3
   To calculate the life path number for an individual born on January 30, 1931:

   Step a. Reduce the full birth date to numbers:
   1/30/1931
   Step b. Add all the digits of the birth date together *individually*:
   $1 + 3 + 0 + 1 + 9 + 3 + 1 = 18$
   Step c. Add the remaining two digits together:
   $1 + 8 = 9$
The life path number for an individual born on January 30, 1931, is 9.

Example 4
   To calculate the life path number for an individual born on January 10, 1900:

Step a. Reduce the full birth date to numbers:
1/10/1900

Step b. Add all the digits of the birth date together *individually*:
$1 + 1 + 0 + 1 + 9 + 0 + 0 = 12$

Step c. Add the remaining two digits together:
$1 + 2 = 3$

The life path number for an individual born on January 10, 1900, is 3.

Example 5

To calculate the life path number for an individual born on September 9, 1974:

Step a. Reduce the full birth date to numbers:
9/9/1974

Step b. Add all the digits of the birth date together *individually*:
$9 + 9 + 1 + 9 + 7 + 4 = 39$

Step c. Add the remaining two digits together:
$3 + 9 = 12$

Step d. Add the remaining two digits together again:
$1 + 2 = 3$

The life path number for an individual born on September 9, 1974, is 3.

Example 6

To calculate the life path number for an individual born on January 13, 1958:

Step a. Reduce the full birth date to numbers:
1/13/1958

Step b. Add all the digits of the birth date together *individually*:
$1 + 1 + 3 + 1 + 9 + 5 + 8 = 28$

Step c. Add the remaining two digits together:
$2 + 8 = 10$
Therefore life path number = 1.
Do not count 0 as a number.

The life path number for an individual born on January 13, 1958, is 1.

Example 7

To calculate the life path number for an individual born on August 3, 1953:

Step a. Reduce the full birth date to numbers:

8/3/1953

Step b. Add all the digits of the birth date together *individually*:

$8 + 3 + 1 + 9 + 5 + 3 = 29$

Step c. Add the remaining two digits together:

$2 + 9 = 11$

Do not reduce further, as 11 is a master number.

The life path number for an individual born on August 3, 1953, is 11.

Example 8

To calculate the life path number for an individual born on April 3, 1932:

Step a. Reduce the full birth date to numbers:

4/3/1932

Step b. Add all the digits of the birth date together *individually*:

$4 + 3 + 1 + 9 + 3 + 2 = 22$

Step c. Do not reduce further, as 22 is a master number.

The life path number for an individual born on April 3, 1932, is 22.

Example 9

To calculate the life path number for an individual born on August 16, 1926:

Step a. Reduce the full birth date to numbers:

8/16/1926

Step b. Add all the digits of the birth date together *individually*:

$8 + 1 + 6 + 1 + 9 + 2 + 6 = 33$

Step c. Do not reduce further, as 33 is a master number.

The life path number for an individual born on August 16, 1926, is 33.

Although it may seem excessive to list nine examples for a somewhat simple calculation, all the possible variations that can occur have been included.

For those who may still be somewhat confused, the following short sentence should clarify any problems:

Keep progressively adding the individual digits together until the total becomes 1, 2, 3, 4, 5, 6, 7, 8, 9, 11, 22, or 33.

Once we have calculated an individual's life path number, we are in a position to define his or her character broadly from that number. The next section takes each life path number and defines positive and negative characteristics, average character traits, physical attributes, home, marriage, and partners, and suitable occupations. So read on and continue with your quest for knowledge into the ancient mystical world of numbers.

3

The Twelve Characters
of Numerology

Characteristics of the Life Path
Number One Person

A Positive One Person
INDEPENDENT, ACTIVE, ORIGINAL,
AMBITIOUS, COURAGEOUS

These people abound in creative inspiration and possess the ability to take others far beyond their normal working limits. This drive and action emulate directly from their enormous inbuilt physical strength. As one would expect, determination features as one of their most common traits, making them a force to contend with both in private and in business life. They are life's natural leaders, with a flair for taking charge of any situation. Since those who have this number possess great originality, it comes as no surprise to find many inventors and innovators born under it. The gift of coupling a unique approach to standard practice provides the golden key to success with this highly ambitious number.

A Negative One Person
STUBBORN, LAZY, SELFISH, DICTATORIAL

Because this basic number is one of power, the negative traits are equally powerful. As a result, these people are inclined to be very stubborn and lazy in both home and business and selfish to the point of being totally inconsiderate of others. Once negative persons of this number have made a decision, nothing ever changes their viewpoint, let alone the admission of defeat or failure. Unfortunately, this character trait drives many negative number Ones to follow the wrong path through to the bitter end, bringing about the downfall of themselves and others associated with them.

An Average One Person

Persons of this type possess all of the above positive and negative traits to a more passive degree, but even average individuals born with this number possess the natural gift of leadership, coupled with the desire to be independent at all times. This leads to a very high percentage preferring to rule rather than be ruled.

Although they make excellent employers, in most cases they make intolerable employees.

Physical Attributes

Strong forceful presence. These people may have a square chin signifying determination and the will to succeed. Clearly defined facial features, coupled with a strong, powerful athletic physique, are common.

Home, Marriage, and Partners

Both male and female of this number prefer to adopt unconventional attitudes toward love, marriage, and home. Life can be exciting living with those of this number because they are definitely not creatures of habit. They abhor system and normal routine; consequently, decisions concerning the home front are usually made very quickly and seemingly without a great deal of prior thought. Due to their definite set of likes and dislikes and their desire to be in charge, marriage and partnerships can be turbulent. Ones usually combine very adequately with personalities less dominant than themselves, thus allowing them to take command of most situations. Unfortunately, choice of partners for this number must be made with a great deal of thought and pretested compatibility. As expected, the combination of two such dominant people may produce disastrous results.

Suitable Occupations

It is natural that those with this number should strive to be self-employed. By doing so they are able to take advantage of their natural attributes to instigate their own decision-making and rise or fall accordingly. It is essential that if they work for somebody else, the occupation be one allowing a reasonable amount of autonomy and freedom in decision-making. If given rein they can produce outstanding results, which, coupled with their physical strength, allows them to work under considerable stress for long periods.

This number makes excellent inventors, promoters, executives, or organizers. They also excel in positions of responsibility within the armed forces, as here their leadership ability can be utilized to the full. Their originality in any field of endeavor will ultimately lead to success.

Characteristics of the Life Path Number Two Person

A Positive Two Person
COOPERATIVE, PEACEFUL, GENTLE,
RESERVED, ANALYTICAL

Positive Twos are extremely sensitive people who possess the wonderful ability of being able to see both sides of any situation. Consequently, they are excellent mediators in any kind of dispute where an unbiased referee is required. Their consideration for the well-being of others is foremost in their minds, which unfortunately leads to them being used by unscrupulous members of the community. They abhor dishonesty and will always be open in their deeds, thoughts, and actions.

They excel in any form of group activity, where their expertise of blending people together can be utilized. A natural progression of these characteristics lies in the ability to be extremely tactful; they make excellent confidants able to keep secrets under extreme pressure. Vastly different from the previous number, Twos are most certainly creatures of habit, preferring standardized, well-proven routine rather than a precarious day-to-day existence. Unfortunately, their reserved manner projects the impression of being aloof, which in most cases is a protective veneer erected to hide their extreme sensitivity. It is pointless to argue with a person born of this number, as their sole purpose in life is to keep the peace, rather than aggravate any situation by disagreeing strongly with any other person's point of view. Their inability or reluctance to dispose of articles and items makes them natural collectors.

A Negative Two Person
INTROVERTED, MOODY, SENTIMENTAL,
OVERLY SENSITIVE, PESSIMISTIC

There are very few completely negative people born of this number, but an apparent trait of those who are is passivity, almost to the state of complete lethargy and apathy, with no desire to enjoy or pursue life. A totally pessimistic attitude could be taken toward any venture, thus alleviating any chance of success. Constant fits of depression and the desire to escape from reality are also apparent, together with the inability to make decisions concerning day-to-day life. Needless to say, a person possessing these negative characteristics would be totally out of place in a position of authority within the business world.

An Average Two Person

These are tolerant, peaceful persons who blend others together, but who have a strong tendency toward indecision and procrastination in business and day-to-day life. These people prefer to be ruled rather than rule themselves.

Physical Attributes

Shy, sweet, demure, slightly inhibited-looking people with a reserved air and aloof appearance. They are usually small in stature and possess clearly defined petite features. They prefer neutral shades that blend in with the background because of their basic desire to remain inconspicuous.

Home, Marriage, and Partners

Their peaceful, cooperative disposition makes them excellent marriage partners. Their aim is to please and they will accept their lot in life without complaint. Females of this number make devoted mothers and wives, being able to cope with the normal home traumas in an unflappable manner. It is uncommon to see any of this number displaying outward signs of affection, other than in the home, as they prefer to suppress their day-to-day emotions toward others. It is utterly essential that Twos live a secure, stable life free from financial worries and burdens. This love of security makes them totally inadequate to handle the worries and upheavals that so often accompany ambitious, go-ahead people.

Suitable Occupations

Any occupation involving group activity. People of this character are natural diplomats, statesmen, psychiatrists, psychoanalysts, or computer programmers. They also prefer fine, systematic detailed work of any nature, provided they are allowed to work away from the normal hustle and bustle of the business world. Twos possess natural rhythm, and any occupation involving music, writing, and poetry would also be suitable.

Characteristics of the Life Path Number Three Person

A Positive Three Person
ARTISTIC, SELF-EXPRESSIVE, EFFERVESCENT, OPTIMISTIC, HAPPY, IMAGINATIVE

Here we find the entertainers of this world, bright, effervescent, sparkling people with a highly optimistic attitude. They are able to cope with all of the many setbacks that occur in life and readily bounce back for more. The ability to bring sunshine into dark places with their very presence is a natural, God-given talent. They abound in good manners and are very conscious of other people's feelings and emotions. The wonderful balance of being able to combine the extreme optimism of number One and the deep consideration of number Two makes this indeed a beautiful number.

Life is lived to the full, often without worry for tomorrow. This basic natural philosophy probably accounts for the inability of those with this number to handle money, as they tend to spend it while they have it. Three is a very artistic number and as such these persons are able to adapt to all facets of the artistic field with natural ease. Their humor is contagious, making them the life and soul of any social gathering. Freedom is utterly essential to this number; consequently the confines of a home or office are not easily accepted. They find it almost impossible to cope with standard routine, but their general manner usually negates any type of humdrum existence.

A Negative Three Person
EXTRAVAGANT, VAIN, NOMADIC

Because this basic number is usually full of the joys of life, the negative counterpart would be totally opposite—far from happy, unable to cope with life, and frequently resorting to escapist tendencies. The inability to settle into one place or one position constantly hinders their purpose in life. Accepting responsibility is hard for a positive person of this number, but almost impossible for a negative one. The natural, uninhibited nature of Threes would be replaced with a superficial two-faced attitude, aimed at using people to their own advantage.

An Average Three Person
The average Threes possess above-average ability in any art form,

encompassing painting, interior decorating, writing, music, and stage. They are happy, inspired people who constantly require the stimuli of similar company. They must exercise caution with finance, remembering to save for a rainy day. Generally their happy and exuberant nature is enjoyed by one and all.

Physical Attributes

Ideally, a person with this nature prefers to dress flamboyantly, using plenty of bright colors. A common fault of this number is to overdress both in choice of clothes and accessories. They love to be the first in the field and wear the latest fashions. Their stature, although not large in proportion, is usually rounded in its effect. Large smiling eyes and high cheekbones radiate happiness and love.

Home, Marriage, and Partners

Pretested compatibility are the key words here, for although positive Three people are duly aware of other people's feelings, the basic desires for freedom, artistic expression, and an uninhibited way of life often pose problems for less extroverted individuals associated with them.

A partner of a positive Three person must possess a sense of humor, a positive attitude toward life, and the ability to adjust to new situations very quickly. If these three points can be adhered to, then life should be a very happy affair. But if the partner endeavors to change the Three personality, suppress or inhibit enthusiasm and humor, or imposes excessive restrictions and limitations, then complications occur.

It is rare to find a truly negative Three as most fall into the positive and average class, for, needless to say, should a person possess negative characteristics they could become very hard to live with. Partners of all Three people should endeavor to exercise some control over the financial affairs of the family, if only to make sure that the bank balance can stand frequent bombardments.

Suitable Occupations

People of this number can be artists of the highest caliber, entertainers, singers, dancers, painters, and actors. Any organizational position is suitable to them, provided it is of a nonbusiness nature and does not require monetary and administrative expertise: beauty experts, cosmeticians, in fact any position that offers freedom of expression, lack of routine, and the stimuli of meeting people.

Characteristics of the Life Path
Number Four Person

A Positive Four Person
TRUSTWORTHY, PRACTICAL, DIGNIFIED, TENACIOUS

This number possesses a positive, scientific, sensible, down-to-earth approach to life and those possessing it can rightfully be classed as the cornerstones of our society. They make excellent organizers and planners, due to their natural ability to evaluate a situation from a practical point of view. Often, they are creatures of habit, preferring the standard routine and system rather than the precarious day-to-day existence of the previous number Three. Loyalty reigns supreme with positive Four persons; consequently, they make excellent marriage partners and business associates, provided all parties are in harmony of purpose.

Four people possess strong willpower, which could be said to border on sheer stubbornness. Once a decision has been made, it will be followed through to the bitter end with a tenacity verging on obsession. Their pragmatic approach to life tends to limit them to a few close friends rather than a large number of casual acquaintances. But friendships made with this number are cultivated for life.

A Negative Four Person
DOGMATIC (TO EXCESS), NARROW-MINDED, REPRESSIVE

The positive attributes of this number are so definite and powerful that the negative traits are extreme extensions of those same characteristics. The negative Four can become completely obsessional and narrow-minded in day-to-day routine, often erasing any opposition or differences of opinion from their minds. Dislike of a person is immediately shown, and no power on earth would change that opinion. They abhor flighty, skin-deep people, and if they are forced to associate with them, disastrous results could occur.

An Average Four Person
These people possess more positive than negative characteristics—however, they all have the common denominator of being practical and down-to-earth. It is essential that both male and female of this number surround themselves with enthusiastic yet practical people. In many cases, this opposite attraction affords a balanced equilibrium that allows Fours to come out of their shell. They should be encouraged to mix and

mingle more frequently, as they are inclined to draw away from others into their own tightly closed shell.

Physical Attributes

Solid build with heavy physical features. Both male and female prefer precise, tailor-made clothing, but fashionably styled. Plain colors are usually preferred, coupled with matching, compatible, and durable accessories.

Home, Marriage, and Partners

Regardless of negative or positive attributes the Four person does not take kindly to fleeting relationships or superficial friendships. They make excellent partners, but need constant encouragement from an understanding partner who is aware of their intentions. They are often overly possessive and will fight to the end if their relationship is threatened.

Below the practical facade lies a highly emotional person, but these feelings are normally always hidden, as they tend to consider highly emotional people as being weak in character. Moderation is practiced in affairs of the heart, and their faithfulness is unquestioned, with the result that given no cause for matrimonial worry or competition, the Four person will be there for life.

Suitable Occupations

Because of their systematic, organized approach, they excel in areas where attention to detail is required. People of this number are good as accountants, economists, instrument makers, manufacturers, or designers. They also excel in military life where precision and systematized routine are essential.

Characteristics of the Life Path Number Five Person

A Positive Five Person
VERSATILE, ADVENTUROUS, SENSUOUS, PROGRESSIVE, HAPPY

These people are always striving to find answers to the many questions that life poses. Here are the true communicators and mixers of this world, as they possess the unique ability to bind people together. Their quest for freedom, both in home and work, often leads to domestic upheaval. Unlike the previous number, these people abhor routine and could never be confined or forced to handle day-to-day tasks, as their motto seems to be "Live life to the full at the moment."

Fives have the natural ability to motivate those around them, which, coupled with a mild but effective aggression, makes them excellent sales people. Love of adventure dominates their lives, and they frequently take pride in tackling the most dangerous tasks with gay abandon. The love of danger and adventure that completely rules this number causes constant frustration to those close to them, who try unsuccessfully to analyze the motives behind these dramatic individuals. Due to their uncanny versatility, they are often multitalented, yet this same attribute can cause lack of direction. Being able to master so many tasks tends to give them an unrealistic attitude toward life, leading to confusion of ambition.

A Negative Five Person
SELF-INDULGENT, AGGRESSIVE, IRRESPONSIBLE, INCONSISTENT

As we have seen with the previous number, negative characteristics are in many cases extensions of the powerful positive force, but to extreme. Consequently, unhappiness and frustration can be experienced by associating with a totally negative Five, who could be completely irresponsible in tasks and decisions concerning home or business life. Fives pursue sensation and freedom with extreme tenacity, making them self-indulgent and totally unaware of the feelings of others around them. The constant search for new horizons and challenges frequently leaves chaos and heartache in their wake. They are able to change their mood and relationship with others in an instant. This inconsistency often brands them as being two-faced.

An Average Five Person
These are fun-loving happy persons who live for today. This outlook, although very commendable, is not often appreciated by other, more stable numbers. Consequently, it is essential that average Fives mix with people of a similar nature to their own. Even the average Five person should be given thought-provoking tasks rather than mundane, day-to-day procedures, otherwise their true potential cannot be realized and utilized. As we have previously stressed, it is not only important that friends and associates be on a similar wavelength, but they should also be prepared for anything to happen, so take heed, for the fainthearted could be overwhelmed with their exploits.

Physical Attributes

As those of this number enjoy the secret of *joie de vivre*, their exterior appearance usually matches their interior sparkle. They are of average stature, and certain features are accentuated. Large, rounded face, high cheekbones, and seductive eyes are common in this number. Their choice of fashions is up to the moment, but not gaudy. They possess the natural ability to make even the drabbest and most casual outfits look appealing.

Home, Marriage, and Partners

Unfortunately, we find a very common factor occurring within the lives of many number Fives. Their sensuous, natural charm offers great appeal to the opposite sex, with the result that they experience more temptations than any other number. Couple this with their love of variety, change, and freedom, it makes their relationships precarious to say the least. Although they are deeply passionate individuals, they find it extremely hard to maintain their feelings for any length of time. This weakness unfortunately leads to many broken hearts, but if their partners are aware of these shortcomings and are able to handle competition effectively, then life with a Five person can be a lot of fun.

Suitable Occupations

Essentially this number should pursue occupations that have direct communication with people, such as in the fields of sales, television, radio, travel, etc. They also excel in the areas of journalism, advertising, and promotion, where media can be used as a vehicle for their expression.

Choice of vocation or occupation is extremely important to these individuals, as it must allow them freedom of expression and individuality. If these character traits are suppressed or inhibited, then their natural talents as communicators and motivators are totally wasted.

Characteristics of the Life Path Number Six Person

A Positive Six Person

RESPONSIBLE, CONSCIENTIOUS, HUMANE,
LOVING, UNSELFISH, TOLERANT

This number is ruled by the planet Venus, therefore love of people is paramount. Children, old folks, invalids, and the infirm are all attracted to their humane, loving qualities. People born with this life path number will fight to the bitter end to protect and uphold justice and the rights of humanity. They abhor skin-deep, false people, as their own love is true and completely natural. As one would expect, they make excellent guardians and parents, being able to treat young folk as small adults rather than immature children.

They are totally aware of the need for love and security within the home; consequently, they will bear any responsibilities on their sturdy and broad shoulders without a word of complaint. Harmony is an essential ingredient in their lives. Harmony of the home, family, business, friends, in fact anyone associated with them. They make excellent companions and can be relied on for help and comfort in times of need. Their extraordinary wisdom and the ability to understand the problems of others commence from an early age, with the result that they often span the generation gap with their friendships.

Their need for depth of physical expression is extremely important, but although the urge is powerful, complete appreciation can only be gained if it is within a fully dedicated, meaningful relationship. Artistic appreciation, together with love of the finer things of life, are enjoyed by this number. Food and culinary ability is considered an art, and as such, indulgence in this pursuit is merely a form of artistic expression.

A Negative Six Person
NERVOUS, CAUTIOUS, JEALOUS, NARROW-MINDED, PESSIMISTIC, INTERFERING

As with other life path numbers, some negative influences represent complete reversals of the positive attributes. Such is the case with number Six, as the true negative person of this number would be vastly different from the loving, humane, tolerant individuals described above. The ability to accept and uphold responsibilities is completely nullified here, because the desire to evade these burdens is foremost within their lives. The giving, humane attitude would be replaced with a selfish, me-first approach that would seek to meddle in and criticize other people's affairs rather than provide sound, logical, honest judgment. A pessimistic attitude reigns supreme, causing considerable unnecessary worry and anxiety over the present and future. A singular attitude is taken toward problems and traumas of home life and relationships, making them depressive people to associate with. Of all the life path numbers, Six rarely produces true negative individuals. Society needs positive people of this number, and nature has endowed the majority of them with an awareness of their purpose in life.

An Average Six Person

These people possess far more positive than negative qualities. Love of home, together with the desire for total harmonious relationships are essential even to average people of this number. All the wonderful attributes and talents of unselfishness and dedication to the well-being of others are enjoyed here, but to a slightly lesser degree, making them more human and realistic in their approach and attitude toward life.

Most average Sixes tend to worry unnecessarily over small minor problems. Major complications are handled rationally and logically, as the answers come directly from the heart. Sixes could never make a decision that endangered or hurt another person's well-being. Thus the need for worry is removed.

Physical Attributes

Medium stature with rounded facial and body features are common with this number. Large eyes and a happy face that exudes magnetism and love. Bright, practical, yet stylish clothes are preferred, with the emphasis placed on individuality and personal comfort rather than the desire to conform to the current fad.

Home, Marriage, and Partners

It is natural for this number to seek loyal, trustworthy partners. The implications of marriage and associations are fully understood, realized, and accepted and furthermore fully upheld. It would be highly improbable for a Six person to enter into a clandestine, fleeting relationship, as this is totally out of character with his or her very being. They work hard to establish harmonious surroundings, realizing that they will probably have to give more than they take. But they give for a specific purpose, and if their loyalty and servitude are not returned by the opposing partner, a protective attitude for what is rightfully theirs will raise its head, creating very powerful negative traits. So be warned, do not tamper or misuse the loyalty or affections of this number. Luckily, Sixes usually find suitable harmonious partners and as such enjoy deep, happy, contented relationships.

Females born with this life path number make excellent mothers, as they possess all the necessary qualities needed for rearing stable, well-adjusted children. Men also possess these same attributes, but tend to be overly protective toward their offspring.

Suitable Occupations

People with this number must choose their occupations and professions very carefully, bearing in mind that their chosen path must be harmonious to their character. Being locked or forced into the wrong vocation could produce negative characteristics. Teaching would be an ideal vocation for those having this number, as here their natural qualities can be utilized to the full. The realization that they are molding and helping the future of the young would attract them to this profession, resulting in the love and respect of associates and pupils alike. Nursing, medicine, child welfare, vocational guidance, and social work would also be suitable occupations for this number—in fact any area in which humanity can be served would be compatible with their nature.

It is worth mentioning that there are a few areas where Sixes must tread cautiously, as their natural attributes, wonderful as they may be, could cause their eventual downfall. Big business, high finance, and sales are three such areas. This is not to say that they could not be successful within these fields, but a somewhat ruthless, self-centered attitude must be adopted to be successful, and this is totally out of keeping with their character. However, experience gained during early working years usually highlights this fact, making Sixes very aware of suitable future areas for their personal endeavors.

Characteristics of the Life Path Number Seven Person

A Positive Seven Person

ANALYTICAL, RESERVED, DIGNIFIED, PEACEFUL,
TRUSTWORTHY, AFFECTIONATE

People born of this number possess an inbuilt spiritual wisdom that often appears to be totally out of character. They are perfectionists in all they do and require others around them to maintain this sometimes impossible standard of perfection. The ability to analyze situations, however complex they may be, abounds within this number. Personal experience is essential to these people, as true knowledge of life's problems can only be gained by experiencing them personally, rather than accepting advice from outsiders. This desire to experience life often causes self-inflicted problems, and the Seven life is usually a series of ups and downs. They rarely possess a wide circle of associates and companions, but friendships made usually last a lifetime. Regardless of their own level of education or social status, they seem to have a deep admiration for learned, intelligent, philosophical individuals and often strike up close, meaningful relationships with them. Their reserved manner is often taken by others as being aloof, which is unfortunate, as this is an exterior facade erected to cover a basic feeling of insecurity.

They frequently experience the desire to be alone with nature, away from people and the hustle and bustle of city life. Seven people find it hard to adapt to twentieth-century existence, so this escape to nature seems to act as a stabilizing influence on their emotions and actions, recharging their batteries, enabling them to cope with present-day conditions. Their profound inner wisdom, coupled with personal experience of life, often leads positive people of this number to become interested in spiritual and occult matters, as here their natural clairvoyance and intuitive power can be utilized to the full.

A Negative Seven Person
SARCASTIC, PESSIMISTIC, LACKADAISICAL, INCONSIDERATE, QUARRELSOME, SECRETIVE

True negative persons of this number would be very hard to live with. Their attitude toward life is one of complete lethargy coupled with a general inconsiderate attitude toward others. As opposed to seeking the answers to life's problems, these people tend to go through life making mistake after mistake, sadly never gaining knowledge or awareness from these errors of misjudgment. They often take the attitude that life owes them a living. If and when they realize that this is not the case, a severe pessimistic outlook takes effect. It is essential to those of this number possessing negative characteristics to realize that they do have a purpose and that this can only be found by living and experiencing life to the full.

The desire to possess the finer things of life without having to work for them is also apparent, often creating a complete materialistic attitude. It would be useless to interfere in the problems of a negative number Seven, as their suspicious nature would tend to look for an underlying motive. Negative traits of any life path number can always be overcome, but unfortunately Sevens have to work a little harder than the rest to achieve the same result.

An Average Seven Person

These persons possess a mixture of both positive and negative traits. Often the average of this number seem to experience a succession of highs and lows within their lives, as stability of living seems to elude them. The desire to gain understanding through personal experience, as opposed to seeking advice and guidance from others, is also apparent. Their frank, down-to-earth approach tends to limit their relationships to a few close friends rather than a whole multitude of casual acquaintances.

Physical Attributes

Short, stocky, powerful builds, with strong facial features, are common. Conservative, quiet, refined clothes are preferred, with emphasis being placed on pastel shades, rather than bright, stunning colors. The perfectionist qualities of the positive side of this number reflect in their appearance, as matching, coordinated ensembles are chosen with great care.

Home, Marriage, and Partners

As with the previous number, Sevens must choose their partners with care. But as opposed to the Sixes who had to place emphasis on the opposing partner, Seven life path people must place the total emphasis on their own capability to sustain a lasting, effective relationship. It is very clear that a person married to a number Seven individual must be prepared to give more than take. This does not mean that Sevens make intolerable partners, but rather that they require more understanding than those of any other life path number. Both the Seven men and women, regardless of negative or positive characteristics, will require autonomy of decision-making and expression within the home. If their opposite partners are prepared to share their interests in life, then Sevens can make excellent husbands or wives.

Suitable Occupations

Any position involving a detailed analytical approach is suitable, such as instrument maker, lawyer, accountant, and computer programmer. Sevens require a considerable amount of freedom within their employment or occupation and will definitely resent or rebel against being told what to do. As employees, they must find suitable areas of employment where their talents can be utilized on an individual basis, as opposed to being part of a team. They tend to be loners, and if left to their own resources can produce the required result. But if goaded into working to a set pattern or schedule, then problems will arise.

Sevens should avoid entering into business partnerships, as their whole character functions as an individual. Their interests in occult and philosophical matters could lead many to seek employment within the field of spiritual enlightenment, as here they can further their desire to look behind the scenes of life.

Characteristics of the Life Path Number Eight Person

A Positive Eight Person
POWERFUL, SUCCESSFUL, INDEPENDENT, CONFIDENT, ACTIVE, FORCEFUL, CREATIVE

This is a very powerful life path number that endows with tremendous potential the positive born within it. These people not only have the ability to conceive far-reaching schemes and ideas, but also the tenacity and independence to follow them through to the end. As you would expect, many successful business people are born with this life path number, as they fully realize the necessity to delegate responsibility, accordingly surrounding themselves with efficient, loyal, experienced associates.

They are very practical people who are aware that success does not come overnight, but that it is planned, organized, and tenaciously pursued. Truly positive Eight persons would find it very hard to accept limitations or restrictions. Luckily, keen judgment suitably equips them to take big gambles with little effort or preconceived preparation. Their confident manner attracts unlimited opportunities, which are eagerly taken, evaluated, and, if worthy, acted on. Concern for other people's opinions and ideals must be exercised by these people, as their singular path in life often excludes the feelings of those closest to them.

A Negative Eight Person
DICTATORIAL, THOUGHTLESS, INTERFERING, MATERIALISTIC, INTOLERANT

As one would expect with a powerful number such as this, negative traits would be excessive extensions of positive characteristics. The wonderful ability to motivate and guide people possessed by positive Eight persons would be replaced with a dictatorial, interfering attitude that would suppress and inhibit the enthusiasm and the efforts of others close to them. Material gains and rewards assume the utmost importance in their lives, often to the total detriment of family, home, and peace of mind. Their dedication to success becomes almost obsessional, and any person who restricts or challenges their supremacy would be ruthlessly dealt with.

It is not surprising that loneliness can be a big problem for negative Eight people. Their singular commitment and dedication tend to alienate them from potential friends and associates. Deep emotional feelings are often suppressed or overruled by a brash, inconsiderate exterior.

An Average Eight Person

Average Eights possess both negative and positive qualities but to a lesser, more passive degree, humanizing the powerful, machinelike characteristics of the positive character. Material gains and rewards are still very important to these people, but not usually to the detriment of their own personal happiness. Organizational ability is very prominent in their lives, but they fully realize that others must also be instrumental in their own personal success.

Physical Attributes

Large and powerful in stature, radiating an air of superiority, efficiency, and competence, Eight people possess excellent taste in matters of fashions and clothes, preferring coordinated colors and expensive materials rather than cheap, gaudy fashions.

Home, Marriage, and Partners

The emphasis on successful associations and relationships with this number must be placed on the opposing partner. We have learned that Eights require freedom of expression and action, not only in business but in matters of the home. Therefore, similar to number One life path persons, it is essential that to effect a happy, lasting relationship, the opposing partner must be less dominant and forceful than themselves. The combination of two equally powerful people could produce constant friction, ending in disastrous results.

A great deal of understanding and consideration must be exercised by those married to number Eight people, as unfortunately, most of the giving and little of the taking should be expected in matters of the home. Dedication to work and business can, with a person of this number, overrule home priorities to the extent that all of the working and many of the nonworking hours could be spent in pursuit of new challenges and business ambitions. Eight people do not make doting parents; they exercise discipline and command respect from their offspring. Consequently, they often experience parental problems during the traditionally troublesome teenage period.

Suitable Occupations

These people excel in the areas of business administration and leadership. They represent powerful, inspired leaders who are able to grasp opportunities very quickly, making the most of every situation. However, it is extremely important that vocations be chosen with a great deal of care. The attributes of this number are so powerful that if their talents are suppressed or given no opportunity for expansion, then an introverted, frustrated person could result.

Finance, commerce, purchasing, contracting, building, personnel work, and law are all suitable occupations for this number. However, these people are better off self-employed and should endeavor to surround themselves with efficient, practical companions. They should exercise caution in management control, and should realize that although they themselves are creative, inspired people, other people's ideas and schemes should also be listened to and investigated.

Characteristics of the Life Path Number Nine Person

A Positive Nine Person
COMPASSIONATE, GENEROUS, HUMANITARIAN,
SYMPATHETIC, PHILOSOPHICAL, TRUSTWORTHY,
IDEALISTIC, SENSITIVE, BENEVOLENT,
ARTISTIC

These trustworthy, honorable people possess absolutely no prejudice. They feel very deeply for individuals less fortunate than themselves and will distribute their humanitarian qualities in face of all adversity to protect or help those in need. Nine is the true giving number. Their generosity knows no limits and they will willingly place themselves secondary to others.

This is the highest fadic (or single digit) number in Numerology; consequently, as one would expect, the attitude and purpose in life of these persons is of a philosophical nature. Material gains are not overly important to these people, although the scales of life frequently reward them for their qualities. This factor is responsible for finding many positive Nine life path people in financially sound positions. Honesty is a fact of life to these people, and misuse of trust given in this area by friends, associates, and companions would cause tremendous friction and loss of confidence, which in most cases would never be regained. Their compassionate nature searches for the problems and worries that sadden other people's lives, with the desire to rectify the situation. People are an open book to positive Nines, as they have the natural gift for intuitive simpatico. However, occasionally, this gift is thrown to the wind if affairs of the heart are allowed to take command.

Their profound understanding of life often manifests itself in the artistic and literary fields. Here they can express their deep emotional feelings through painting, writing, sculpture, or some other suitable art form. They rarely conform to the normally accepted boundaries within these areas and will frequently surprise everyone by creating a totally new artistic experience. The positive Nine person makes friends very easily, as people are attracted to their magnetic, individual personality. They possess many wonderful talents, of which the most rewarding is their profound gift of understanding people, which if used correctly can be of so much benefit to the well-being of others.

A Negative Nine Person
IMPATIENT, DICTATORIAL, INSINCERE,
INCONSIDERATE, OVERLY EMOTIONAL, INDISCREET,
IMPULSIVE

Whenever we find extremely strong positive characteristics, we must also expect to encounter equally strong negative tendencies; such is the case with Nine life path people. However, most Nines fall into the categories of positive and average, rather than totally negative, but for those in question the following points would apply: A selfish attitude toward life replaces the benevolent, generous traits of the positive type. Here the desire to help others is completely overruled by the need to help themselves alone, often to the total detriment of family, home, and friends. People are expected to jump when negative Nines give orders, and they become very impatient if their instructions are not followed with precision and speed. The understanding of others is completely nullified, as their dictatorial attitude seeks to command rather than to listen, thus disrupting any harmony in working conditions and often causing alienation from personal associations.

Companionships and friendships are usually restricted to people with a similar attitude to their own, with the result that they invariably lead a lonely life. True lasting success cannot be gained by a negative Nine person, as rewards will be of a short-lived, material basis rather than one of peace of mind and spiritual happiness.

An Average Nine Person

These people possess far more positive than negative qualities, but like so many other life path numbers, to a more passive or human degree. The average of this number still possess extremely compassionate tendencies. The desire to help others, especially the troubled or underprivileged, is recognized, as is their trustworthy, honest approach to life.

The greatest single common denominator that stands out with the average of this number is a lessening of their intuitive powers. The positive Nines use all of their wonderful talents without apparent loss or suffering themselves, but unfortunately the average Nine often leads a life of being used and let down by others. The desire to understand individuals is very strong, but they seem unable to handle this attribute effectively. Their extreme generosity is often misused by others, causing frequent personal financial problems. However, the scales of life reward these people with an abundance of enthusiasm and peace of mind.

Physical Attributes

Tall stature is common, together with a lean, sometimes undernourished look that accentuates Nines' facial features. They exercise discretion in their choice of garments and invariably prefer fine, subdued material to gaudy, flamboyant colors.

Home, Marriage, and Partners

Nines, as many other life path numbers, must choose their partners with a great deal of care. People are attracted to their magnetic personality, but it is essential that intended partners be fully aware of the Nines' totally generous nature, which could often jeopardize family financial affairs, as they come to the aid of someone in need. Here lies a very big problem for most Nines. If they combine with a person similar to themselves, they will enjoy a happy, harmonious, loving relationship that will last forever. But materially, their life will suffer, especially if one or both is an average Nine person. On the other hand, if they combine with a down-to-earth, materially conscious individual, problems will arise quickly, as these generous qualities will only be appreciated within the home and not outside. Such is the cross that Nines must bear, and it is for them to choose, depending on the rewards they seek in life. Nines make excellent parents, although they must guard against spoiling their offspring, again due to their overly generous nature.

Suitable Occupations

The natural attributes of Nines can be successfully utilized within the areas of medicine as doctors, nurses, psychiatrists, or chemists. They also excel in literary and artistic fields and could be suitably employed as journalists, publishers, and publicity agents. But to take real advantage of their humane, giving attitude, Nines should always seek to be involved either full- or part-time in areas of welfare. Here they can escape the normal business world and concentrate on understanding and helping individuals less fortunate than themselves. Negative Nines should endeavor to be self-employed, as here decisions can be made individually and without consultation with others, leaving them to rise or fall on their own merits.

Characteristics of the Life Path Number Eleven Person

A Positive Eleven Person
INTUITIVE, AVANT-GARDE, IDEALISTIC, VISIONARY, CULTURED

Eleven represents the first double number of Numerology, and as twenty-two and thirty-three, they are referred to as the master numbers. The attitude toward life of those with this number is extreme; consequently a positive Eleven person possesses the above key attributes to a far greater degree than any other single number.

These people are truly stimulating individuals, who signal the way for others to follow. They are deep-thinking people who constantly endeavor to unravel life's mysteries. As such, it is not unusual to find many positive people of this number, propounding individual, well-thought-out theories on spiritual, religious, and occult matters. Material gains are not important to people of this life path number, as realization and appreciation of the finer free things of life hold far greater significance. Their inventive abilities should always be given free rein, which together with their natural intuitiveness can often produce startling results.

Other people look to these individuals for guidance and direction, as they exude complete individuality of person and purpose. Their idealistic attitude that seeks to conquer and reform the world has to be somewhat refined to fit in with current society. However, their grandiose humanitarian schemes often contain a great deal of down-to-earth common sense and simple logic.

Artistic expression is extremely important in their lives and often reflects their innermost feelings and desires, although a somewhat avant-garde result usually eventuates. A positive Eleven, although not a true leader of people, is a leader of minds and ideals. Before action must come the concept, and herein lies the true worth of these visionary people.

A Negative Eleven Person
SARCASTIC, THOUGHTLESS, INTROVERTED, MATERIALISTIC

Elevens are powerful people; consequently, the negative characteristics of this master number must be tempered, otherwise they could become their own worst enemies, eventually leading to their own downfall. The wonderful visionary qualities of the positive character are completely missing from the negative persons, as their introverted, pessimistic nature thinks only of the past and allows no consideration for the future. This preoccupation with past problems often nullifies any opportunities that arise, with a result that life often takes on a downward, ever-decreasing spiral until complete apathy results. They can be extremely thoughtless in their dealings with other people, constantly suspecting or mistrusting anyone prepared to help them in their endeavors. As a result they often become very embittered, lonely people who often wonder why they have few close friends. A sarcastic attitude is also evident, again caused by their failure to recognize or accept the help of friends and associates.

A truly negative Eleven person is very materialistic, with absolutely no consideration for spiritual rewards. Thus, peace of mind often eludes them throughout life. Luckily life does not produce many totally negative Eleven people, as the vision and inspiration used to guide others also guide themselves.

An Average Eleven Person

These people are far more positive than negative in their approach to life, but tempered to a more passive degree. Intuitive powers are still acute, but tend to suffer from lapses and indecision. Others still look to them for guidance and direction, although it is common for the average of this number to experience problems with their own personal direction.

Average Elevens often fall into the trap of using their visionary powers to create utopian, nonworkable schemes that they, let alone others, would find impractical to maintain. Spiritual rewards still hold greater individual significance than material gains, as does the need for unusual artistic expression. They must guard against becoming dreamers in their attitude toward life, realizing that dreams are intangible, whereas life is tangible.

Physical Attributes

Small stature with petite features are common to people born of this number. They prefer fashionable, tailored garments made of beautiful, vibrant, smooth materials. They exude beauty and fully realize that appearances can enhance their inspirational attributes.

Home, Marriage, and Partners

Positive and average Elevens make excellent partners and parents, as they fully realize the need to give more than they desire to take. However, it is very important that the opposing partner be on the same wavelength as themselves, otherwise their humanitarian, visionary attributes will create the opposite reaction within their own home environment. Partners must be prepared for a somewhat avant-garde, unusual, yet exciting existence. Elevens conceive new concepts and ideas in a flash, and their impetuous enthusiasm radiates to all concerned.

Problems will arise if the opposing partner is a materially conscious person, as this is totally out of character with the beliefs and ideals of Elevens. They make excellent parents, fully realizing that the training of infants is a dedicated responsibility, and they uphold this task admirably. As you would expect, the Eleven household places enormous emphasis on spiritual rewards and the helping of others. Therefore, children raised in this environment invariably receive a balanced, well-adjusted upbringing.

Little can be said for the home environment and partnerships of a totally negative Eleven, except that the partner needs to be extremely tolerant and understanding to cope with the many traumas that will invariably arise. It is worth mentioning here, that realization by Elevens of their own negative or weak traits is the first step to correction. Reformed individuals usually become extremely powerful and positive as a direct result of living both ends of the scale.

Suitable Occupations

The artistic field offers suitable vocations for those of this number, provided they are not made to conform and produce standardized results. Given autonomy, they can create the unusual and sometimes impossible. For here their true inspirational qualities can be utilized.

Eleven people excel as artists, costume designers, window dressers, fashion coordinators, beauty specialists, and hair stylists. The teaching and legal professions also offer tremendous challenges for people of this number, for here their infectious, enthusiastic, visionary attributes can be used to the full. Any position that involves motivating and inspiring others would be ideally suitable.

Elevens seeking to be self-employed should follow these guidelines: First, the type of business or profession must be chosen with a great deal of care. Second, they must surround themselves with down-to-earth, logical business confidants. Third, the financial affairs of the company should be handled by a qualified accountant. Last, decisions relating to company expansion or ventures should not be taken individually but as a team effort. This last point is mentioned, as although it seems contrary to the normal visionary powers of the Eleven person, we know that the average of this number tend to create idealistic, nonworkable concepts. Thus, by sharing the decision-making with other, more down-to-earth associates, schemes and concepts can be adopted to become workable and viable propositions.

Characteristics of the Life Path Number Twenty-two Person

A Positive Twenty-two Person
POWERFUL, SUCCESSFUL, ARTISTIC,
EMOTIONALLY CONTROLLED

This is the most powerful of all life path numbers in Numerology and people with the positive attributes of this number possess tremendous power from within. They can reach any heights in life, as they recognize absolutely no limits. They are the master planners of this world, possessing the ability both to conceive grandiose, far-reaching schemes and to carry them through to the end.

Their capacity is unlimited and as such they can achieve enormous success, prestige, fame, and glory should they desire. Few people born with a Twenty-two life path number possess truly positive character-istics; most tend to fall into the average group where these powerful at-tributes are somewhat tempered. Those who are lucky enough to possess these characteristics usually take full advantage of them, realizing very early in life that they can achieve so much with so little effort. It is com-mon to find these people devoting their lives to schemes that are benefi-cial to mankind. Here they can exert their true superiority and leadership on a grand scale without limitations. Spiritual understanding is common with other life path numbers; however, Twenty-twos are unique in that they not only possess this profound attribute, but couple it with an emotionally controlled attitude toward life. This natural gift automati-cally provides a purpose in life for these people—that of motivating and guiding others toward worldly peace, happiness, and understanding.

A Negative Twenty-two Person
MATERIALISTIC, DICTATORIAL, INSENSITIVE, OVERBEARING, OBSESSIONAL

A totally negative Twenty-two person is rare. Twenty-two is the most powerful of all three master numbers; therefore the wonderful heights that can be reached with a positive Twenty-two person are often replaced with the very depths of despair for a negative individual. How-ever, for the very few totally negative people born of this number, the following points apply: A completely insensitive attitude reigns supreme, as they use their latent powers for total individual gain regardless of any hurt they cause in the process.

This search for material gain often becomes so powerful that the laws and rules of society are utterly ignored. Dictatorial by nature, they will neither listen to nor act upon others' advice, preferring to exert complete authority and be in command of each and every situation. Their lust for power is obsessional, and they will go to any lengths to reduce or nullify the opposition.

It is worth mentioning that the laws of life often apply to this num-ber. The dividing line between love and hate, genius and insanity, is as thin as the line between the truly positive and negative Twenty-two person. Experience has shown that the negative of this number often reach a stage in life when, due to some specific situation or circumstance, their course or path in life is changed overnight. Thus, many true posi-tive people of this number have often commenced life following the negative path. The natural power exists, but the choice and use rest on the individual.

An Average Twenty-two Person

These possess both negative and positive traits but to a very much lesser degree. However, even the average of this number have the natural ability to reach great heights within their chosen life path. Being able to control their emotions obviously equips them admirably for the political and business fields, where wearing the heart on the sleeve can signify instant failure. Unfortunately, we must somewhat generalize with this number, as so many paths are open to these individuals that a natal chart analysis is absolutely essential even to ascertain negative or positive qualities. However, suffice to say, it is a wonderful number to possess and should be used not for total individual material gain, but for the good of mankind.

The world needs humanitarian "Twenty-two" people to show the way to peace and happiness, so that we may follow in their guiding light.

Physical Attributes

Tall in stature, with an air of superiority and efficiency, which is sometimes considered aloofness by others. It is uncommon (except with a negative Twenty-two) to find these people overweight. They exercise extreme restraint and would never intentionally abuse their body. They realize that a healthy body provides the only effective vehicle for personal success. Their choice of clothes is perfection plus, as they take a great deal of care and consideration with their exterior appearance.

Home, Marriage, and Partners

As one would expect, partners for Twenty-two people must be chosen with a great deal of consideration and their compatibility pre-tested to see if the opposing partner is prepared to live the type of life chosen by these people. Obviously compatibility depends on positive, negative, and average characteristics, but the common denominator of all three types of Twenty-twos is the necessity for their partners to share, encourage, endorse, and maintain the life-style chosen by their mate.

Interference is never taken lightly and restrictions are definitely not accepted. It follows as a matter of course that home finances will not present problems. The Twenty-two man is a good provider and will consider the feelings of his spouse by assuring adequate finances without burdening her with knowledge of the enormous business gambles he invariably takes.

As parents, Twenty-two people must devote time to their offspring. The tendency to become totally involved in their chosen field of endeavor can often lead to avoidance of home responsibilities. The Twenty-two woman invariably involves herself in community welfare work, where her talents for organization and efficient control are in great demand, sometimes, however, to the detriment of her own home and family.

Suitable Occupations

From their attributes and generalized character traits, it is apparent that the future of Twenty-twos should lie within the areas of business, politics, and community welfare. Whatever profession or vocation is chosen, they must have autonomy of decision-making and freedom of control. Many areas are suitable for these people, but invariably as their talents become recognized, they climb the ladder of promotion until they gain complete control. This succession of promotions usually takes an amazingly short space of time.

Self-employment offers by far the best vehicle for their talents, since there would be no limitations and restrictions imposed by others. The artistic field also offers tremendous challenges, as their practical, yet creative, nature can often turn hobbies into lucrative vocations. Twenty-two persons are indeed multitalented and can master almost anything they set their minds to. This is a wonderful attribute to possess, provided one realizes that competence can be achieved in a multitude of subjects, but genius can only be achieved by specialization.

Characteristics of the Life Path Number Thirty-three Person

A Positive Thirty-three Person
HUMANE, EMOTIONAL, HIGHLY SENSITIVE,
DEPENDABLE, TRUSTING, LOVING,
COMPASSIONATE

A number Thirty-three person is similar to the Six life path individual, but possesses extreme combinations of the positive and negative character traits. Therefore, this resume should be read in conjunction with the Six life path number description.

The total emphasis of those having this master number lies in their extremely loving nature. They strive for justice and will protect the little man or woman regardless of personal consequence. They are tolerant, dependable individuals who can be relied upon to carry through a task from beginning to end. Identical to the Six person, harmony is extremely important to their well-being, and they will willingly sacrifice their own desires and ambitions to create harmony within the home and at work.

As you would expect, they are highly sensitive and emotional people and invariably wear their heart on their sleeve. Thirty-threes are an open book to any intuitive individual. They enjoy a multitude of lasting, loving relationships, but unfortunately, also suffer many severe hardships in matters of the heart and finance. With their trusting nature, they take people at complete face value, thus presenting golden opportunities for unscrupulous individuals to take advantage of them. Thirty-threes are at their best when dealing with children, old folks, and the infirm, for here their compassionate nature is able to understand fully the problems and worries affecting these individuals.

A Negative Thirty-three Person
NERVOUS, INTROVERTED, OVERLY EMOTIONAL,
HIGH-STRUNG, OVERLY PHYSICAL

Again, similar to negative Six people, the attributes of these individuals are very powerful and represent complete opposites to the wonderful positive characteristics. Luckily, with all master numbers, the majority of people fall into the average category. However, the true negative Thirty-three individual would be very nervous, high-strung, and possibly introverted by nature.

The emotional powerhouse harbored by all Thirty-three people turns inward with the negative of this number, creating a highly jealous and overly emotional individual. They find it almost impossible to think and reason logically, spreading their talents in all directions. This in turn can create severe frustration that manifests itself in fits of depression and the desire to escape from reality. But here again, the line between positive and negative is very thin, and often negative individuals of this number change their attitude toward life overnight. Overemphasis on physical desire is a common trait with the negative of this number.

An Average Thirty-three Person

Average Thirty-threes possess far more positive than negative characteristics, but again, somewhat more humanized and less angelic. Harmony is essential to these people: harmony of home, work, associates, and companions. Similar to the Six life path person, they would place their desires secondary to the creation of a happy home environment. They usually enjoy a large circle of friends, all with similar characteristics to their own.

They abhor violence in any shape or form and would go to any lengths to avoid a confrontation that could result in physical exchanges. Thirty-threes possess a natural affinity with animals and will often walk where angels fear to tread within these areas. They are life's natural worriers, who invariably spend a great deal of time worrying over the smaller, nonimportant, day-to-day problems. However, when major mishaps and traumas arise, they can be relied upon to keep calm and carry on in the face of adversity.

Physical Attributes

Thirty-threes mostly are of medium stature, with a tendency toward slight overweight (usually caused by their love of food). Bright, harmonious, stylish clothes are usually preferred.

Home, Marriage, and Partners

Experience has shown those of this number are the easiest to live with, as their loving, tolerant nature seeks only to create peace and harmony, provided, however, the opposing partner is able to return the necessary amount of emotional and physical love.

They frequently need to be assured that their relationship is successful and meaningful. This stems from a basic feeling of insecurity, coupled with the need for love and reassurance. Thirty-threes will often experience temptations in matters of the heart. Although they are basically loyal individuals, they are ruled by their heart and can often mistake other people's flirtatious innuendos as being true expressions of love and desire. This temporary lapse of loyalty often occurs if they are experiencing problems within their own existing relationship.

Thirty-threes make excellent parents. They realize the need to devote time to their offspring, so consequently they organize their lives accordingly. The tendency to be very easy with their children is common, with the result that problems frequently arise during their children's adolescence.

Women of this number make excellent mothers, being able to understand and fulfill the needs and desires of their young. The desire to protect their offspring from the worries and problems of life is also common with both males and females of this number. They must realize, though, that sooner or later their children will be exposed to the cold, hard world and that if they have not been fully prepared, problems could result.

Suitable Occupations

Experience over the years has conclusively proven that Thirty-three people should avoid being involved in big business and finance. Their attributes, wonderful as they may be, are definitely not suitable to the dog-eat-dog existence of present-day business. Therefore, more emphasis should be placed on occupations or vocations of a spiritual, nonbusiness nature.

Teaching, nursing, child welfare, veterinary or social work would all be suitable areas for Thirty-three persons. If they are aware of their strengths and weaknesses, much happiness and fulfillment can be gained from the correct choice of vocation. However, if they are desirous of entering the world of business and finance, it is utterly essential that they surround themselves with strong, trustworthy people who can act on their behalf within their areas of personal weakness.

4

The Day of Birth

In Chapter 2 we learned how to calculate an individual life path birth number utilizing month, day, and year of birth. By doing this we were able to categorize people into twelve distinct areas, outlining their positive, negative, and average traits, home environment, physical attributes, and suitable occupations.

We expressed the opinion that the definition of a birth number was only a complementary factor to the total analysis gained by compiling a natal chart. In the next chapter you will learn how to compile this chart and to interpret the aspects formed within it. But now we must enlarge upon the interpretations of each number, to include character traits applicable to each day of the month. It is a simple process to take the day that a person was born and match it to the following descriptions.

Do not reduce the day of birth to a single or master number, as each particular day possesses an individual significance. These day interpretations should be added to the conclusions gained from the twelve life path birth numbers.

Characteristics of the Thirty-one Day Numbers

Numerological Day of Birth: One (1)
Example: 8/1/1942

Strong willpower is evident, coupled with independence and exceptional analytical ability.

Better planners than builders, these people possess an active mind ruled more by logic than emotion. They are practical, idealistic persons who are capable of devotion to causes and people. This number does not produce demonstrative individuals. It is important to encourage them, and although they enjoy a sensitive, independent spirit, they must learn to express the great latent energy and power within them.

Numerological Day of Birth: Two (2)
Example: 9/2/1953

These people are emotional, sensitive, and intuitive. They make friends easily and are popular with others, yet they often portray a nervous air when in the company of large groups. People appreciate their warmhearted nature and emotional understanding that cries out for affection and love.

They must beware of becoming depressed and moody, as this turns their emotional awareness inward, causing anxiety and mental turmoil. Unfortunately these people find it very hard to bounce back to reality when depression sets in. They should enjoy the somewhat Taurian characteristics they possess, of desiring comfort and material luxury. Music, group activity, dancing, poetry, and other fields which nourish their talents are advisable.

Numerological Day of Birth: Three (3)
Example: 4/3/1926

This artistic day number indicates *joie de vivre* and vitality of life. Threes have an ability to recover quickly from setbacks or illnesses encountered in home or business. Restlessness is evident with those having this day number, and they should endeavor to cultivate outside interests completely different from their normal business routine.

They often portray an easygoing, sometimes couldn't-care-less attitude. The natural ability to express themselves in front of audiences makes them excellent stage types, much sought after in social gatherings and society functions. Often affectionate in nature, they go through many upheavals and crises in matters of the heart, but manage to overcome these traumas with the same speed as they occur. Three is an excellent imagination number, which obviously combines beautifully with their talents.

Numerological Day of Birth: Four (4)
Example: 6/4/1943

All earthy attractions show up in Four birthdays, especially love of the country and its natural way of life. As with Sixes, their love of home and family life is paramount in their lives. They have an affinity for such hobbies as sculpture, music, and painting.

They must beware of an Eight tendency to dominate or impose their will on others, which, if taken too far, could be termed intolerant. Expressions of love are somewhat limited, due to their inability to express their innermost desires. A sense of humor is important to those with this day number, and they should try at all times to maintain surroundings of a happy nature, attempting to undertake pleasurable pursuits in hobby and leisure activities. They must learn to digress occasionally from standardized and regimented routine to include a little lighthearted nonsense in their daily lives.

Numerological Day of Birth: Five (5)
Example: 1/5/1939

These people possess versatility in all areas of life. But they must learn to temper this natural ability and localize their energies rather than become a jack-of-all-trades and master of none. They prefer and usually do associate with lively individuals who possess the same extroverted nature and love of variety and freedom as they.

Their infectious, sparkling manner attracts and stimulates others to produce their best efforts. Consequently, this attribute should be utilized fully within certain business fields. Unfortunately, this love of life and freedom makes them precarious marriage partners, who must learn to consider the feelings of those close to them.

Numerological Day of Birth: Six (6)
Example: 9/6/1928

This day number indicates humanitarian persons who seek to find the good rather than the bad points in people. Happy, harmonious surroundings are absolutely essential to their well-being. They are life's natural givers, dispensing spiritual love to one and all, but often receiving little in return. Luckily, they have the ability to forgive and to open their hearts to other people's shortcomings. This capacity to love obviously produces a firm basis for marriage and friendships. They will give far more than they expect to take and are compatible with most types of individuals.

Children are attracted to them, as they are able to communicate on a noninfant level and involve these younger ones in day-to-day activities and conversations. These Sixes have a tendency to worry to excess; ironically, major problems are tackled with comparative ease, while minor disturbances are often magnified beyond all proportion. Harmony is essentially their keynote; consequently, music should provide the best outlet for their natural ability.

Numerological Day of Birth: Seven (7)
Example: 4/7/1944

These people should always investigate new ventures carefully and seek to avoid deception in business matters. This is a number indicative of patience and Sevens can often play a waiting game with exceptional results.

Their set ways do not make them easy people to live with. They should learn to relax more and make a special effort to commune with nature and meditate during each day. These people frequently desire to be alone with themselves at least some of the time each day. This seeks to counteract the distractions and possible negative influences of others with whom they associate.

This is a testing number that often burdens its holders with obstacles throughout life. It is essential that they gain knowledge from these adversities, thus allowing them to impart their wisdom to others in need.

Numerological Day of Birth: Eight (8)
Example: 9/8/1952

People born with this day number make ideal businessmen or businesswomen, as they are able to conceive on a grand scale and plan accordingly. They should try to own or direct their own business. They should also be wary of forming partnerships, as others rarely share their ability or desires to conceive and plan on a huge scale.

They are scrupulously honest and can always be trusted to handle money in a logical and discreet manner. They are idealistic people and possess a philanthropical streak that allows them to devote some of their valuable time to worthwhile causes. Because they are able to appreciate and utilize their talents, limitations are rarely experienced. Thus they have the potential to rise to the very top in most fields of endeavor.

Numerological Day of Birth: Nine (9)
Example: 12/9/1952

Many people will benefit from the humane efforts of those born with this day number. Sadly, the desire and ability to help others are often not reciprocated, with the result that they are frequently used and abused by one and all. They must take extreme care in their choice of career or vocation, as their open-mindedness leaves them vulnerable to deceit.

These people often experience frustrating one-way marriages that invariably find them giving all and getting very little in return.

The artistic fields offer wonderful opportunities to those of this number, as their lack of business acumen is unimportant.

This is a beautiful day number that realizes fully the need to help others. It is sad that these qualities are often abused by unscrupulous individuals.

Numerological Day of Birth: Ten (10)
Example: 4/10/1954

This is a fortunate vibration, showing a good mind, determination, and the will to succeed.

Those born on the tenth day are creative people with the ability to promote any idea, as long as they believe in it. They abound in variety and possess the natural ability of being able to handle a multitude of tasks at the one time. They must guard against becoming workaholics and should cultivate an interest in music or art as a form of mental and physical relaxation.

As in number Three, these people have considerable prana vitality and speedily recover from ill health.

They must not let home affairs overburden them, as this could reduce their ability to keep hold of their many business reins.

Numerological Day of Birth: Eleven (11)
Example: 5/11/1945

This is a master day number that often shows a tendency toward erratic personal behavior, being up one minute and down the next.

These people are high-strung and inclined to be nervous, but this tendency is often balanced by their strong intuitive gifts. They must learn that in achieving success the weaknesses and failings of others must be understood. They should make a conscious effort to keep in good health, thus building a barrier against the effects of nervous energy.

Numerological Day of Birth: Twelve (12)
Example: 2/12/1929

This number shows a great love of life, coupled with the desire for action. Possessing great magnetism and imagination, those of this number have the ability to change other people's opinions to suit their own line of thought.

Their mission in life is usually fully known and realized, and as such their gift of imagination steers them adequately on the right course to success. However, their life seems to follow a series of highs and lows, mostly caused through their desire for immediate action.

They are inclined to be distracted by tempting affairs (not necessarily romantic); these should not be succumbed to, as their line of direction and ambition could be sadly affected.

Numerological Day of Birth: Thirteen (13)
Example: 4/13/1949

Far from being unlucky, persons with this birth day number have excellent managerial potential, with the ability to motivate and stimulate others to work beyond their normal capacity.

Real estate features very strongly with these people, as it offers a natural vehicle to utilize their management ability to produce lucrative rewards. Anything to do with the earth, such as mining, geology, building, or construction, is definitely suitable for a person born on this day.

They should endeavor to show more readily their hidden nature of loving; otherwise, misunderstandings can occur in their close family relationships. Their stubbornness often hides a good logical mind, but they must learn to listen rather than to dominate conversations.

A harmonious home environment is essential for their well-being, as they are unable to work under emotional stress, often taking work problems home and vice versa.

Numerological Day of Birth: Fourteen (14)
Example: 9/14/1932

These people possess a prophetic nature which combines harmoniously with an ability to reason things out on a down-to-earth, matter-of-fact level. They should be advised to pursue an artistic hobby, if only to distract them from their natural gambling instinct, which, if not controlled, could produce disastrous results. However, they have a flair for business on a grand scale which can be utilized to its fullest when self-employed.

Due to their doubtful choice of friends, this number attracts many hangers-on who find it relatively easy to take advantage of their trusting nature. They should beware of the entrapments of physical desire purely for its own sake and should avoid the temptations of excessive alcohol, drugs, and barbiturates.

This is a very powerful number, which if misused, could be destructive to themselves and others close to them.

Numerological Day of Birth: Fifteen (15)
Example: 1/15/1937

This is an excellent, harmonious vibration. Deep study does not usually appeal to these people, but luckily they are able to absorb subjects and learn with comparative ease.

Financial success is possible for them, as their attractive nature often leads to lucrative situations and opportunities being offered to them. Their understanding nature, together with their ability for dedicated self-sacrifice, makes them loyal and worthy subjects for any deserving cause.

Music often exerts a profound influence on these people, and they should utilize this as a form of mental and physical uptoning. They are generally fond of life and realize that maintaining a correct balance of health is necessary to their existence. Their generous, charitable nature guarantees close, everlasting friendships.

Numerological Day of Birth: Sixteen (16)
Example: 3/16/1940

These people must control a basic tendency to become irritable with other people. This, when combined with an aloof nature (their weak point), could cause disruptions among those closest to them. People born with this day number cannot be told what to do. They intensely dislike interference from others and will, if provoked, erect a mental barrier that will completely ignore the suggestions or person in question.

Unfortunately, they tend to take the attitude that others should always come to them, with the result that if this weakness is not rectified, a lonely life could result. If they learn to open their minds and hearts to the world, then people will be attracted to them freely.

Numerological Day of Birth: Seventeen (17)
Example: 4/17/1957

This is an excellent number for banking interests and general financial affairs. Great success is promised in these pursuits if persons with this number can become less set in their ways and learn to unwind. They should try to use their lofty minds and proudness of spirit to help manage the affairs of others.

A contrary indication in their Numerological profile shows gaining of profit followed by loss and a scattering of what they have secured. This process often occurs throughout their lives. This can be avoided if associates are utilized to censor, moderate, and bring down to earth their somewhat grandiose schemes.

They are, incidentally, doubters of occult subjects but should learn to keep an open mind even when proof is seemingly lacking.

Numerological Day of Birth: Eighteen (18)
Example: 4/18/1946

People born on this day often become associated with vast community efforts, where their natural gift for administration can be enjoyed.

Usually their first attempt in any particular field is not successful. They must learn to continue their efforts, realizing that success will eventuate if one pursues it long enough. They possess a strong intellect but often shy away from the advice of others. Luckily, their judgment and reasoning are sound. However, they should at least listen to others' opinions, even if these are not acted upon.

Problems connected with marriages and friendships often occur, however. These can be overcome if they dedicate themselves to making these close associations work. Effort is needed and effort must be made.

Numerological Day of Birth: Nineteen (19)
Example: 4/19/1933

These people can rise to great heights and then fall swiftly to great depths if they allow emotion to overrule their gifts of logic and perseverance. Their versatile natures can enhance their success in many pursuits, including medicine, law, art, and the field of music.

They frequently possess an inherent carefree nature, although this is not necessarily displayed openly. Despite their nonconformist attitude, they respect responsibility; therefore a political career could provide an effective vehicle for their original minds.

They are continually striving for a higher and a better way of life and would detest being kept down or inhibited in a mundane, nine-to-five vocation. Those close to them should be aware of this character trait, preparing themselves for difficulties that could occur as a direct result.

Numerological Day of Birth: Twenty (20)
Example: 2/20/1948

Working with others in a small business or in a friendly, sociable atmosphere would attract those born on this day. By letting others plan life's grandiose schemes, they are able to retain their "I'm happy doing what I am" attitude, without any conflict.

They usually prefer to express themselves in the written, rather than spoken word, although they are by no means inarticulate. Their Numerological profile indicates a well-educated person who is sympathetic and affectionate toward others.

They are not really the manual labor type. Although they like to live close to nature and enjoy the open-air life, hard physical work does not appeal to them.

Unfortunately, mental pursuits are usually associated with city life, so it is important that frequent revitalizing trips to the country are made by people born with this day number, if only to provide a much needed mental break.

Numerological Day of Birth: Twenty-one (21)
Example: 9/21/51

These people possess a natural aptitude for dancing, as well as a gift for the other arts. Their fine voices could be used equally as well in public speaking or singing.

It is essential that partners of this number realize that frequent expressions of love and desire must be shown toward them, as they are inclined to suspect loss of interest or waning of love for them.

They have a good mind and educational pursuits would be advantageous to them, especially where instruction of others is required, such as teaching or vocational guidance.

The tendency to worry excessively, usually over minor problems, often makes them flighty, nervous, moody people. They must learn to express their desires and problems rather than keeping them bottled up inside, thus magnifying them out of all proportion.

Numerological Day of Birth: Twenty-two (22)
Example: 5/22/1965

This is a master day number that can bring about extremes of nature; consequently, balance must be aimed for at all times.

Those with this number experience frequent ups and downs that are usually caused by nervous and physical overaction. Luckily, this mental and physical exhaustion can be balanced and moderated by taking plenty of rest and relaxation away from the normal hustle and bustle.

They are fortunately blessed with a strong intuitive ability and can often safely act on first impressions.

They often experience never-ending battles between acting out their ideals and trying not to overstep the limitations imposed by society and those within it. This dilemma can be resolved by realizing that their personal ambitions must be subjugated on behalf of others, on a universal level. This, in fact, is the great mission of this powerful master number. Twenty-twos can and frequently do succeed in any field that fulfills their highest ideals. Innovators, artists, musicians all feature strongly among this day number.

Numerological Day of Birth: Twenty-three (23)
Example: 5/23/1943

These people possess a sympathetic, understanding personality, and must progress through life utilizing their gifts for the service of mankind. They are intuitive people, able to understand the needs of others, and would be ideally suited to the fields of medicine, nursing, and psychiatry.

Their down-to-earth attitude does not readily apply to artistic fields, as they consider these pursuits nonessential to daily life.

They are independent, self-reliant people who are able to work and live unaided by others. This strength of character attracts to them others less dominant. Consequently, they are often instrumental in providing the motivational or catalystic influence to other people's eventual success.

Numerological Day of Birth: Twenty-four (24)
Example: 1/24/1941

This is an action day number and as such these people abound in energy. This is a tremendous attribute if used correctly and suitable creative outlets can be found, but if abused, a noneffectual, restless person could result.

Dramatic in deed and nature are these people; therefore above-average success can be expected in the entertainment industry. This over-dramatization unfortunately carries through in all they do; consequently, wasted energy and hyperactivity can be experienced in day-to-day life. Living with a person of this day number can be both exciting and frustrating, as his or her life can change direction from day to day. Therefore, their partners must possess great understanding and patience and be prepared to flit from one trauma to another.

The basic tendency to indulge in fits of depression is there, but rarely experienced, as their flamboyant, extroverted nature suppresses this negative instinct.

Although they are domestic creatures and seek the joys of a happy home environment with children around them, they find it hard to knuckle down to a life of giving and placing themselves second to their offspring. If this problem offers a threat to their career, then deep-down, previously suppressed negative traits will come to the surface.

Numerological Day of Birth: Twenty-five (25)
Example: 3/25/1950

This day number shows heightened intuitiveness to the extent that often people born on this day possess both an interest in and a gift for the occult field. Unfortunately, although this wonderful attribute can offer help to the community, their own affairs often suffer as a result. They can succeed in business if they harness their powers of concentration to counterbalance a tendency toward haphazardness.

In matters of love, these people should endeavor to overcome a tendency to wear their hearts on their sleeves. Their affections often go overboard, completely negating their normal intuitive instincts. Consequently, they should try to practice what they preach.

Their self-expression can often take an art form, since they are naturally gifted in painting, pottery, and sculpture.

This again is a testing day, and people born within it often experience greater setbacks and difficulties than the average. Experience produces wisdom, and life can only be learned by living it. Therefore, as life progresses, their strength usually increases and weaknesses diminish, with the result that spiritual and material rewards usually come late in life.

Numerological Day of Birth: Twenty-six (26)
Example: 8/26/1957

These people must learn to forget what has happened in the past and realize that the present and the future are of greater value.

Although they may not have enjoyed a thorough education, they are aware of the benefit of such and as a result will make any self-sacrifice to enable their children to receive the opportunities that they themselves missed.

The ability to harness a creative, nonbusiness talent and turn it into material success is apparent with this day number; consequently, the artistic fields offer great rewards for their entrepreneurial expertise.

Similar to other day numbers, these people must learn to capitalize on success. Their tendency to spread their interests too far can often negate their ability to reap the rewards of life, thus producing frequent highs and lows in their financial affairs.

Love of home and children is very important, but they must allow their offspring individuality and freedom of choice rather than insisting on a dominating parental control.

Numerological Day of Birth: Twenty-seven (27)
Example: 5/27/1925

The Numerological profile of these individuals indicates a forceful, determined personality that can tend to be erratic by nature.

They do not take easily to direction by superiors and should in most situations seek leadership themselves.

Wanderlust tendencies often dominate their lives; consequently, their choice of vocation or business often involves travel.

They have a rather passionate nature, which at times can be over-done. This is most strongly indicated within the home.

Their versatile nature provides a valuable aid in artistic pursuits, as they are able to recognize future trends and act accordingly. Although literary talents are clearly indicated, the tendency to ramble and digress from the basic theme is also very apparent.

This is a powerful number that can experience extreme conditions. However, knowledge of this fact, together with correct choice of vocation, can often temper these powerful forces.

Numerological Day of Birth: Twenty-eight (28)
Example: 10/28/1950

Love and affection dominate the life of those born with this day number. Their inherent strong willpower and dominant personality tend to magnify situations out of all proportion. But these adverse tendencies can be overcome by clear-cut actions and forgetting unrealistic day-dreams and trivial affairs.

A sense of freedom is essential, as limitations and restraints placed upon them can cause very real anxieties and suffering.

They should cling to their ideals regardless of what is happening around them.

Numerological Day of Birth: Twenty-nine (29)
Example: 5/29/1934

This again is an extreme day number and as a result frequent highs and lows will be experienced throughout life. Vision and inspiration can work to the benefit of the holder, yet they can often create severe problems in the present. These people must learn that the future relates directly to the efforts of what they are actually doing now.

They are not easy people to live with, as their ups and downs can be somewhat nerve-shattering to those close to them. Extreme happiness and elation can often be followed by severe depression and moodiness.

A good home is essential to those with this number, as it provides a solid, stabilizing base to their normally precarious existence.

Greatness nearly always emanates from mental extremities, so these people possess the natural ability to excel in certain areas of life, usually where the good of mankind is the dominant theme.

Numerological Day of Birth: Thirty (30)
Example: 9/30/1943

These people must beware of a basic bombastic streak and realize that they are not always right. Their imagination and intuition must be fortified with a greater sense of wisdom that should be gained from the pursuit of knowledge. They make excellent teachers and social workers.

They are loyal and reliable, though not above dallying into casual flirtations. They should beware of possible tendencies toward laziness and avoid placing too much importance on being praised for their positive deeds and achievements. They enjoy strong recuperative powers; thus, they usually enjoy healthy, well-balanced lives. However, one area of danger for this number lies within occult fields. Their constitutions and mental programming do not equip them with the necessary strength to maintain equilibrium in these dangerous areas.

They make excellent companions, but a little more care must be taken when choosing them as lifelong partners.

Numerological Day of Birth: Thirty-one (31)
Example: 5/31/1967

People born on this day also experience extremes within their lives, and as with other similar examples must learn to capitalize on their basic talents and strong character traits.

These people possess excellent managerial and business capabilities, and they will be successful provided they also recognize and use the talents of those around them.

Friendships are very important to them, and although not great in number, they are maintained for life. They seldom forget a kindness or injustice, and readily help those in trouble.

Creative writing can often provide a suitable outlet for their self-expression, especially if this literary talent is utilized within the more down-to-earth nonfiction field.

They often have financial difficulties, but if a forceful attitude is taken, then these problems can often be totally overcome, or at least lessened.

The fear of loneliness, especially in latter years, frequently haunts people born on this day and they tend to worry unnecessarily about the future. If they open their hearts and live for today, tomorrow's dream will become a reality.

5

The Amazing Method
of Pythagoras

Tuning In to the Vibrations

If we remember back to Chapter 2, the question of people fitting into twelve character types was raised and the answer was given that the birth number was important, but that it was only a contributing factor to the total accurate analysis.

By now you should have mastered the art of calculating a person's life path number. So now we take you much deeper into the ancient world of numbers, explaining how we arrive at various conclusions and character traits. It is this method that has enabled us to astound and amaze countless thousands of people at shopping centers, radio and television shows, and lectures. By using this method, a finely attuned degree of accuracy can be expected. But before gaining this accuracy, one must be prepared to practice over and over again the steps given in this chapter.

By utilizing the ancient Pythagorean method, we are able to tune in to a person's vibrations simply by knowing their date of birth. This knowledge allows us to dissect a person's innermost feelings, desires, strong points, weak points, and health. In fact we will be in the unique position of being able to combine many professional services into one basic system—the system of numbers. Seems impossible? Well, let's find out how.

We must realize that many factors influence a person's life: our parents, education, friends, and associates. These influences sometimes work for our benefit, but other times they work against us; consequently, people may not appear as they are. Numerology provides us with a template for any individual untouched by human hand or will, unchanged by circumstances, and devoid of mass influences. It is this natural individuality that we seek to define. Unfortunately, as you progress in your studies to become a Numerologist, you will become aware of the same sad fact that we have experienced for many years: that ninety percent of people are, first, not using their natural birth talents and, second, they have not even taken the time or effort to find out what they are.

Between us, we hope to correct this sad situation.

Construction of the Pythagorean Triangles

Every person has a date of birth, consisting of the month, day, and year numbers, and it is from this date of birth that an accurate basic natal chart can be compiled. There are nine fadic (single-digit) numbers plus zero, from which all other numbers emanate. Consequently, we use a double triangle system to divide these nine basic numbers into set areas.

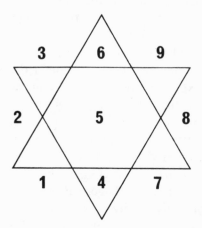

Each area within these triangles has a corresponding number. As we can see, the numbers commence from left, progressing up; i.e., number 1 is in the bottom left corner, 2 is above the number 1, and 3 is in the top left-hand corner. Number 4 is placed in the middle lower section, with the numbers 5 and 6 immediately above. The 7 is situated in the bottom right-hand corner, with 8 and 9 directly above it. This configuration gives us a perfect chart, which of course is totally impossible, because an individual could not possess a birth number of nine single digits.

As we learned in the chapter that dealt with the calculation of the life path number, zero does have a significance in Numerology, but it does not have a place within the natal chart.

It is now a simple exercise to dissect a person's birth date and place the individual numbers within their respective areas of the double triangle framework. Let's look at some examples from various dates of birth.

A person born on 4/13/1942
would possess the following chart:

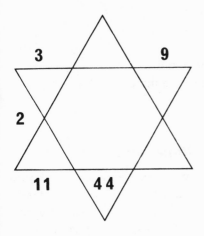

A person born on 6/10/1950
would possess the following chart:

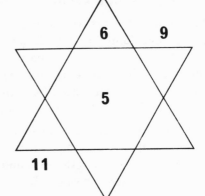

A person born on 8/18/1949
would possess the following chart:

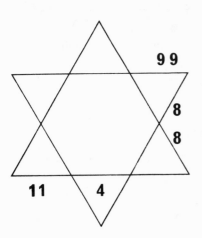

A person born on 4/23/1957
would possess the following chart:

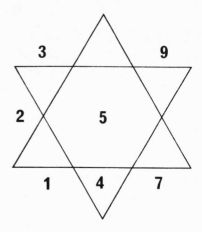

If you practice this chart compilation for a few days, you will be amazed how quickly you can place the numbers in their corresponding areas. Practice makes perfect applies adequately to the subject of Numerology.

Single, Multiple, and Missing Multiple Numbers

You will notice as you compile your own chart and those of your friends and family that each one of them has blank areas. It is impossible to possess a perfect chart with a number in each area. Generally speaking, where there are numbers missing, it signifies apparent basic weaknesses that can often be corrected by other number configurations. Where a multiple of numbers appear in any one given area of the double triangle strengths, extremes or an imbalance can occur, but this again can be tempered by other aspects within the chart.

Many Numerologists expound the theory that balance is to be desired in any chart. This must be true to a degree, but from our experience, greatness often emanates from a totally unbalanced chart.

The subject of single, multiple, and missing numbers will be dealt with in greater detail later in this and the next chapter.

Interpretation of Areas
Within the Pythagorean Triangles

Now that you have become adept at compiling the basic chart, you must learn how to interpret each single and multiple line of numbers shown within the triangles.

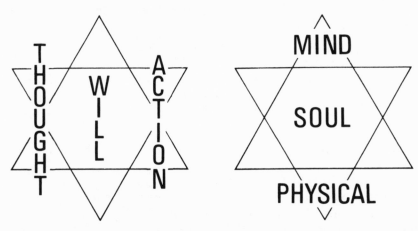

Each of these charts has been segregated into three distinct areas, showing clearly how each full line has a natural significance. Numbers 1, 2, and 3 are associated with thought, 4, 5, and 6 with will, 7, 8, and 9 with action, 3, 6, and 9 with the mind, 2, 5, and 8 with the soul, and lastly 1, 4, and 7 with the physical body.

We will now look at each individual line for its basic meaning.

One, Two, and Three (1–2–3) Thought Line

This indicates a person's creative imagination process and the ability to conceive ideas, thinking ahead to their eventual fruition. It is also associated with thought concerning the community and the well-being of others. It is wise to remember that thought always precedes action; consequently, a harmful thought can be just as mentally and physically detrimental as a harmful deed or action.

Four, Five, and Six (4–5–6) Will Line

This line is a natural progression from the thought line. What has been conceived can now be molded and planned within this line. It reflects the will to succeed in the conceived task.

Seven, Eight, and Nine (7–8–9) Action Line

What has been conceived and planned can now be put into action. As we know, some people abound in creative inspiration but are unable to plan their ideas effectively or put them into action. Likewise, other people are not gifted with the ability to conceive ideas but are able to plan upon other people's concepts. This line shows the ability to put the thought process into physical action.

It can be seen from the preceding three lines that they are all in perfect orderly progression. The thought is originally conceived, it is then streamlined and planned, and eventually put into practice or action.

As we learned previously, it is impossible to possess a perfect chart, as it is equally impossible to find a person who has succeeded without the help of others. Experienced businessmen and motivators realize the importance of surrounding themselves with people who possess ability in areas that they themselves are weak.

Let's now look at the other three lines: mind, soul, and physical:

Three, Six, and Nine (3–6–9) Mind Line

As opposed to the thought line, which expresses our creative ability and the innermost thoughts concerning ourselves and the well-being of others, the mind line expresses the actual mental talents, such as the level of intelligence, the ability to rationalize one's thoughts, and the degree in which imagination can be utilized in everyday life. The thought line expresses our innermost feelings which are mostly kept within us, whereas the mind line expresses the outward mental activity that is seen and heard by all.

Two, Five, and Eight (2–5–8) Soul Line

This line represents the center of all being, both individually and universally. Although it is referred to as the soul line, it is more aptly named the "innermost emotion area," for it is here that our unique individuality is expressed both inwardly and outwardly. The soul combination rectifies the imbalance of our thoughts, especially where other people are concerned. This is achieved either by modifying our thoughts and actions to include and consider others, or by strengthening them to assist ourselves alone. These two opposite reactions depend on the strength or weakness shown in an individual natal chart.

One, Four, and Seven (1–4–7) Physical Line

This line deals simply with the physical adequacy of the body to carry through the processes of the previous mental combinations. It shows level of health, stamina, and the ability of the body to maintain a level of healthy, harmonious existence. It also houses the mental computer of our body and mind, storing experiences and likes and dislikes that obviously affect our very day-to-day existence.

The astute reader will now begin to realize why Numerology expertly defines our character. It is this age-old art of dissecting the innermost mind—a mind that is uncluttered and unprogrammed by society, outside influences, or circumstances—that has made Numerology a thought-provoking subject for thousands of years.

It can now be seen that the study of numbers places more emphasis on the creative ability of the mind rather than the physical manifestation of a society-programmed human being. We will see in later chapters how this knowledge can set in motion the wheels of action within a person—wheels that will transport a person from the being they are into the being they should or would like to be. Later chapters will show very clearly the steps that must be taken to equip ourselves to live in harmony with our very being.

Let us recap our experience so far. We now know how to calculate a number and the basic interpretation of this number, how to construct a natal chart and the definition of the lines shown within the chart.

There are two ways to become a Numerologist. The simplest way (but not the best) is to refer to this book at all times while compiling an individual's chart, writing down on a sheet of paper the aspects shown. The second way, which is obviously much harder, is to read, reread, and read again all of the aspects and interpretations so that you are able to compile a chart actually in front of a person without reference to this or any other book.

I must express an important viewpoint at this particular stage of your learning. Numerology, like most other occult subjects, deals exclusively with an individual. It is therefore of prime importance that you reach a level of experience prior to compiling other people's charts. A little knowledge is dangerous, but a little knowledge in the wisdom of Numerology can be very dangerous indeed.

Interpretations of the Individual Aspects Formed by the Numbers Within a Person's Date of Birth

The previous section explained how to compile a natal chart based on a person's date of birth, clearly showing how to dissect the individual digits and position them within the double triangle configuration. We must now look closely at each digit and multiples of same to see how they define definite character traits. It is essential for the student, prior to reading and learning these interpretations, to understand fully the chart construction and number positioning.

With each single, double, triple, or more aspect description, we have included an illustration of a chart configuration that applies to each heading. Remember that the character traits apply only to the number in question; therefore ignore the other shaded areas within the charts.

ASPECTS FORMED BY THE NUMBER ONE

Single One (1)

Example: Date of Birth 4/9/1952

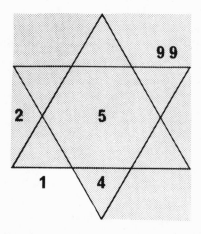

This signifies a gift with words, either of the written word or more commonly the spoken word. The ability to express themselves in a forthright manner is apparent in these people, but this does not apply to expression of innermost feelings. These persons have an inherent difficulty in being able to unfold their mind and converse on subjects that hold a deep personal significance for them. This single aspect shows a basic tendency to speak as one person without the consideration of other people's points of view. A defect of speech or even the tendency to talk too fast is often shown. Basically this number shows outward expression rather than inner spiritual fulfillment.

Two Ones (1 1)

Example: Date of Birth 3/15/1938

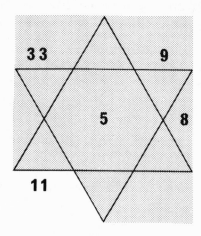

The eloquence of the single One is also found here, but with one very important difference. Whereas single Ones express themselves in a singular manner, the double combinations have the ability to understand both sides of a situation. They possess the natural trait of adapting another person's point of view to suit their own, making it sound as if it originally came from them. This is a well-balanced combination which, if used correctly, could be a tremendous asset.

Three Ones (1 1 1)

Example: Date of Birth 1/12/1940

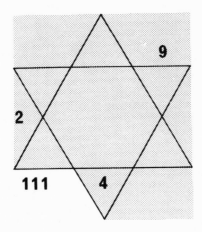

Writing talent is shown very clearly here—the ability to use words to form lucid mental pictures, which would appeal to the majority of the reading public, makes the triple Ones excellent authors and journalists.

Unfortunately, some of this number combination find it difficult to express themselves clearly in speech. Their minds are working at such a great pace that their mouths find it hard to keep up; consequently, they are often branded as chatterboxes. This factor can often be detrimental, as the world does not produce many good listeners. But basically, triple Ones are bright, happy people who are strongly advised to mix with their own type and avoid moody people.

Four Ones (1 1 1 1) or More

Example: Date of Birth 1/11/1929

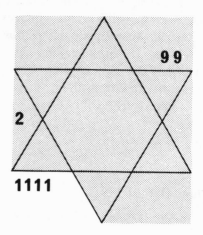

Example: Date of Birth 11/11/1946

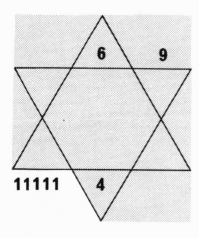

Example: Date of Birth 12/11/1911

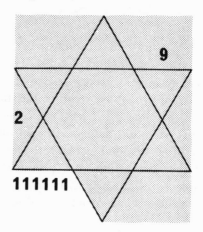

Example: Date of Birth 11/11/1911

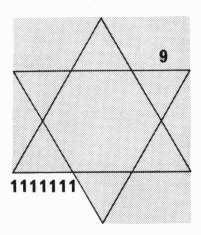

This clearly indicates an overtaxing of physical and mental energy. This type of person finds it extremely difficult to relax and turn off. They are constantly pushing themselves on both the mental and physical plane. Speech expression is extremely strong, to the extent of being overbearing in discussions and differences of opinion. Because of their speed of thought and action, confusion can exist between thought and expression, which often results in misunderstandings with other people. The combination of five Ones or more can indicate an overly physical person with strong basic desires and a possible leaning toward violence. This often occurs where the sequence of Ones is in a follow-on manner, as 11/11/1926.

Extreme combinations of Ones can also point to obesity, overindulgence, and the desire to eat the wrong types of food. This is a very strong aspect that needs a creative outlet for this pent-up energy. If an outlet is found, a happy, powerful, alert, and successful person would eventuate. But if a suitable outlet cannot be found, then a self-centered, moody, aggressive individual could result. From our experience, we have found many people with this strong combination of four or more Ones to be inwardly powerful but outwardly confused.

The literary and artistic fields are ideal outlets for this pent-up energy. Generally, these people throw themselves into any task with enormous vigor and determination, thus often achieving dramatic results in an amazingly short space of time.

ASPECTS FORMED BY THE NUMBER TWO

Single Two (2)

Example: Date of Birth 2/14/1949

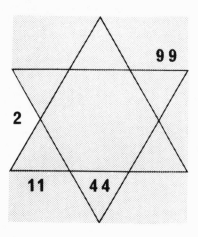

This single number possesses the ability to detect insincerity in others immediately, which usually results in them forming firm opinions on people at first meeting—luckily these opinions are rarely wrong. They are sensitive and intuitive people, but this sensitivity often makes them prone to emotional hardship. They must learn to control deep emotional feelings, as it could affect their physical well-being.

Two Twos (2 2)

Example: Date of Birth 6/23/1952

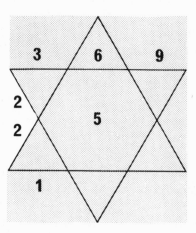

This combination shows heightened sensitivity and intuitiveness—but ironically enough, although possession of these traits is strengthened, those who have them invariably associate with doubtful characters and people who use them for their own advantage. They are often accused of putting the wrong people on pedestals and of ignoring true friendships in favor of superficial relationships. Their intuitive ability can work both for them and against them. Being able to be perceptive about others is a wonderful gift if used constructively, but frequently it is used to hurt and offend others close to them. They must at all times guard against becoming involved in other people's problems, as their extreme emotional character would, in most cases, influence their advice.

Three Twos (2 2 2) or More

Example: Date of Birth 2/20/1962

Example: Date of Birth 2/22/1932

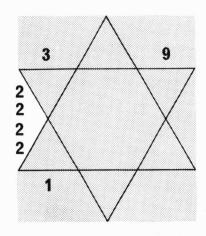

Example: Date of Birth 2/22/1922

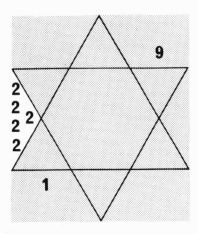

Confusion or frustration reigns supreme with this powerful combination. Unfortunately, they find it almost impossible to control or temper their extreme emotional sensitivity, with the result that they often drift along on a cloud of their own, completely oblivious of the world around them. This self-induced escapism seems to be a release mechanism instigated by nature to act as a buffer against the hardships of life.

It is essential that those closely associated with a person who possesses this combination be aware of this basic imbalance and to endeavor to alleviate this by frequent shows of affection, guidance, and love. Those whose triangles have three Twos or more must avoid the tendency to take things to heart, as they will take even generalizations as a personal affront. This character trait often leads people with this configuration to become loners with few close friends. Again, as found in other extreme combinations, outlets for pent-up feelings must be discovered, otherwise mental frustrations would eventually manifest themselves in physical ailments. The ideal outlet for this number combination would be in the field of music.

ASPECTS FORMED BY THE NUMBER THREE

Single Three (3)

Example: Date of Birth 10/28/1931

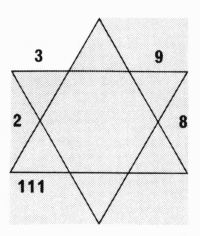

This number possesses great creative imagination and the ability to conceive far-reaching yet practical ideas. These people are equipped to cope with challenges and the problems of day-to-day life, as they have the natural ability to take the optimistic rather than the pessimistic approach. They are morally strong and will protect and aid close friends throughout life.

Two Threes (3 3)

Example: Date of Birth 8/30/1953

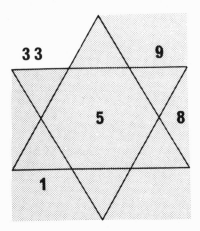

This indicates a nonconformist and a person who would go out of his or her way to complete a mundane task in an original or different manner. Writing talent is often evident, due to the fact that one with this combination possesses great imagination and the ability to express thoughts into words. The nonconformist attitude can frequently be an unsettling influence on a double Three, and he or she has to learn that society and people within it must abide by a certain amount of conformity.

Three Threes (3 3 3) or More

Example: Date of Birth 3/13/1943

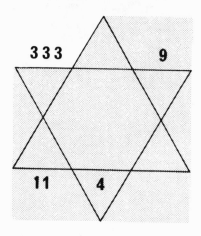

Example: Date of Birth 3/3/1933

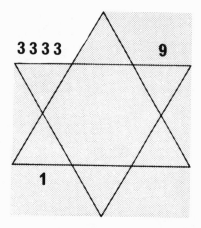

Strong mental ability is enjoyed by those having this combination, but they must avoid becoming too absorbed within their own thoughts, thus excluding the wealth of knowledge to be gained from others. With this extreme combination, the tendency to become too self-centered and a dreamer is very apparent. They should refrain from being too argumentative, which is often due to their inability to listen to other people's points of view.

Basically the number Three is a happy number, but as it is the last number of the thought line and the first number of the mind line, it is essentially occupied with a person's mental capabilities. Therefore people possessing this multiple combination should use this natural attribute to the full. However, they must learn to come down to earth if only for brief periods.

ASPECTS FORMED BY THE NUMBER FOUR

Single Four (4)

Example: Date of Birth 12/14/1960

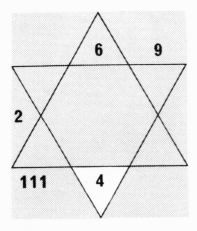

This single number shows a practical, down-to-earth person who possesses the gift of organizing others around them—provided this organization is of a noncreative nature. The combination of a highly creative person with another possessing this number is excellent, because where one conceives the other plans. These people are invariably talented with their hands and are especially gifted in handicrafts. This number also indicates a leaning toward music and could produce accomplished musicians, who would take to learning their chosen instruments with organized determination.

Four is a material number; consequently, those whose number it is must avoid becoming too conscious of worldly chattels, realizing that spiritual rewards are far more significant.

Two Fours (4 4)

Example: Date of Birth 4/14/1938

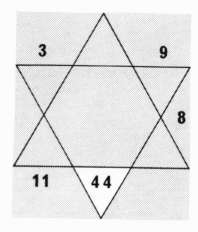

Excellent organizational ability is shown in this combination, together with the desire and the will to complete a task from the very beginning through to the end. Tremendous ability with the hands is also evident, both in work areas and as a hobby. Consequently, double Fours would be ideally suited to the arts of sculpture, pottery, metalwork, and silverwork. Accuracy is of prime importance to these people; they abhor generalizations and vague statements. It is worth remembering when dealing with persons of this number combination to present accurate assessments and statements to them, as they are meticulous with their own dealings and require others to act likewise, especially in the field of business.

Tidiness is very important to them, possibly because they realize that confusion and scruffiness can lead to inaccuracy. They frequently experience severe restrictions within their lives. Some Numerologists consider this to be detrimental, but we are firmly convinced that because of constant restrictions being placed upon them, there is a strengthening of character, thought, and deed.

It would be unwise for others to try to suppress these people, as much more can be gained by mental and spiritual encouragement.

Three Fours (4 4 4) or More

Example: Date of Birth 4/14/1934

Example: Date of Birth 4/4/1944

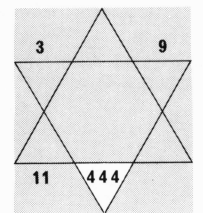

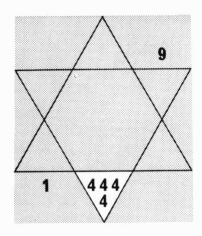

This combination signifies confusion, as the attributes and character-istics can work both for and against the recipient. The triple Four com-bination always indicates an ability with the hands almost to the point of genius. But, unfortunately, it is very rare to find these people using this powerful natural talent. Restrictions that occur with the single and double Four are increased in magnitude here, so, a person must be strong enough to overcome these enormous burdens. They tend to be set in their ways and find it very, very hard to vary from established routine.

The general organizational ability of Fours must be tempered, as they could become slave drivers and tyrannical in their approach to life and business. As we have found with all other triple number combina-tions, outlets for talents and energy must be found; otherwise severe frustration will occur. The suitable release valve for this combination lies in practical, artistic use of their hands, especially in the music or handicraft field. This activity, though, must be of a high physical nature, rather than one of mental or passive tasks.

ASPECTS FORMED BY THE NUMBER FIVE

Single Five (5)

Example: Date of Birth 3/12/1954

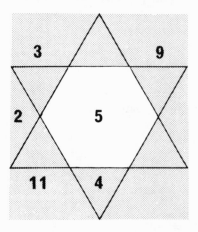

This single number is one of the most important within the whole chart, as it represents the "mixing" number. It is placed within the center of the Pythagorean Triangles; therefore it applies to all the other areas that surround it, influencing the thoughts, actions, and deeds of all the other aspects. The unique trait of being able to motivate others can often provide the catalyst to other people's success. Due to their great strength and determination, they are able to push other people beyond their normal limits.

This is an independent number that requires freedom not only in expression, but in business and home life. Frequently people with this single number attract domestic strife and upheaval. It is unfortunate that although they can be of so much benefit to others, they are often at a loss to correct or solve their own problems.

Two Fives (5 5)

Example: Date of Birth 5/15/1937

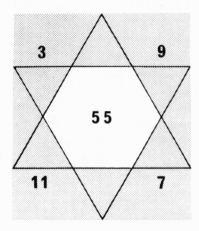

Singly Five is a very powerful number; therefore multiples increase that power in direct proportion. Persons possessing this configuration would be extremely strong in character and able to impart their will onto others with astounding ease. Domestic upheaval is heightened with the addition of another Five in the chart, making these people very hard to live with. They must not allow this powerful dormant energy to manifest itself through abuse of the body in alcohol, drugs, and sexual prowess. Sensuality is increased with this combination, and as a result, they must learn to channel their excessive physical desires into other more creative areas.

Freedom is absolutely essential to these people; they allow it in their associations and expect other people to do likewise. It is important that anybody associating with this number combination be aware of these basic character traits.

Three Fives (5 5 5) or More

Example: Date of Birth 5/15/1935

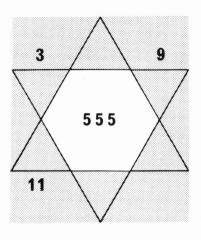

Example: Date of Birth 5/25/1955

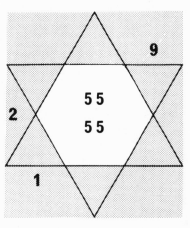

This is sheer power personified that few people would be physically or mentally equipped to handle, but luckily it is a configuration that rarely occurs. Tremendous drive and initiative are shown here, which, if used correctly, could be responsible for the holders of this quadruple number achieving anything their heart desires. But if used incorrectly, frustrations and anxieties could arise and manifest themselves in a similar fashion as shown with the double Five. They must learn to take a long-term approach to life and not expect miracles to happen every day. They make dynamic individuals, with the ability to adjust and tackle any task with ease. Inordinate love of adventure is shown very clearly with this configuration; consequently, they would be inclined to tackle the most hazardous tasks without one second of thought. They offer no explanation for this love of danger. To them it is part of life, but unfortunately, others find this hard to accept.

ASPECTS FORMED BY THE NUMBER SIX

One Six (6)

Example: Date of Birth 4/12/1946

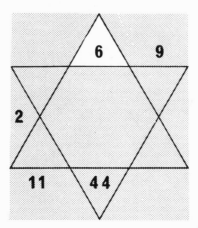

This number signifies love of the home and its environment. Persons with this number are adequately suited and equipped to bear the responsibilities of family life and the many ups and downs associated with its normal, day-to-day running. Their ability to establish and maintain a natural rapport with children and old people makes them excellent parents and guardians. Harmonious family life is essential to the single Six, as worry over marital and family problems may negate their ability to fulfill daily chores or work. The desire to be totally absorbed within a family unit often stems from a basic feeling of insecurity and a fear of being alone in life.

Two Sixes (6 6)

Example: Date of Birth 9/6/1926

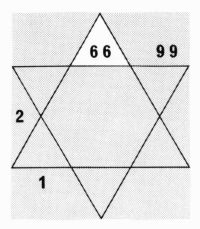

Those with this double number often experience anxiety within the home that frequently follows them through life, commencing with overly protective parents and then occurring again, when they themselves are parents.

When individuals experience extreme conditions during their childhood, they frequently dedicate themselves to creating the opposite with their own family. These people are inclined to be too involved and immersed in family activities. They must learn to exercise balance and allow others close to them to live and grow with a certain level of independence. Unfortunately most people born with this configuration are unable to learn this rule of life, with the result that they frequently experience emotional and physical disturbances.

Three Sixes (6 6 6) or More

Example: Date of Birth 6/16/1916

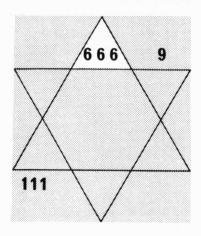

Example: Date of Birth 6/6/1966

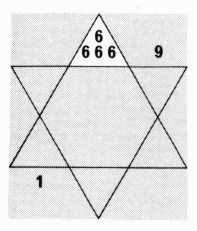

It is essential for persons possessing this triple number combination to realize that children do grow up and that in time they will leave and form their own family unit. Although this may seem a hard fact to accept, it is imperative that they do so, otherwise their overly protective instincts will create problems within the home.

Their complex nature frequently prefers the pessimistic approach rather than one of happy optimism. This, unfortunately, creates very-mixed-up people who often go out of their way to find problems, causing unnecessary worry for themselves and those close to them. One who is of this extreme combination requires an outlet for this pent-up emotional energy. This can often be found in various hobbies where a creative approach is desired.

ASPECTS FORMED BY THE NUMBER SEVEN

Single Seven (7)

Example: Date of Birth 7/24/1931

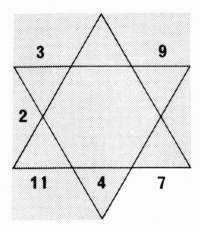

This number signifies self-denial and sacrifice. These people must realize that when problems occur, they are being tested for their strength of character to overcome them. Unfortunately, many of the difficulties experienced are self-inflicted, with the result that they have to work so much harder than the average person to achieve a worthwhile result. One very important point to remember is that experience makes life's most effective teacher. If a problem has been overcome, then the answer is already known, should it occur again.

Two Sevens (7 7)

Example: Date of Birth 4/17/1927

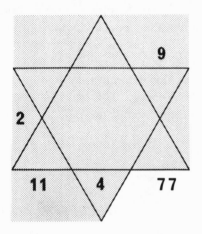

This combination signifies great inner strength and the latent ability to overcome life's frequent obstacles. Those having these numbers possess a gift of being able to analyze situations. This talent should be utilized to its fullest advantage, as this often provides the golden key to their own innermost problems. This testing combination produces understanding and wisdom, enabling them to pass on the benefit of their knowledge in spiritual and material matters for the good of the community. This configuration often indicates musical ability.

Three Sevens (7 7 7) or More

Example: Date of Birth 7/17/1927

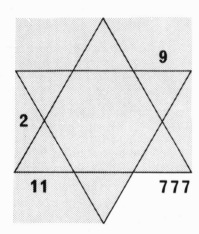

Example: Date of Birth 7/7/1977

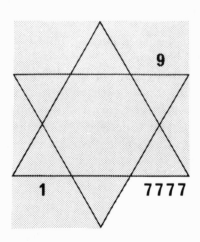

This extreme configuration is a progressive extension of the double number, but with more emphasis placed on the ability to delve into the very nature of the universe, exploring its problems and defining its purpose.

It is common for people possessing this single and multiple configuration to show interest in the areas of psychic research and the occult. They must, however, note that extreme caution should be taken when seeking further knowledge in this field. It is also essential that prior training and guidance be given by qualified individuals to equip them with the necessary awareness to tackle this far-reaching subject.

These people must face up to the tasks at hand and never shirk away from them. Their burden in life is usually so great that accepting defeat can produce a profound demoralizing effect on their well-being; whereas success can provide the stimulus and motivation to achieve anything within their grasp.

ASPECTS FORMED BY THE NUMBER EIGHT

Single Eight (8)

Example: Date of Birth 9/23/1938

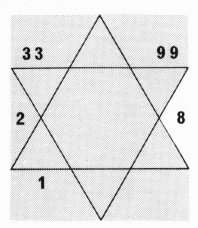

Most people born with this single number are tidy and methodical, yet surprisingly enough they rarely finish tasks at hand, preferring to stop halfway. It is common for these people to experience considerable restlessness and the desire for constant change. This tendency should be controlled, as they could become rolling stones that never gather any moss.

Two Eights (8 8)

Example: Date of Birth 4/28/1928

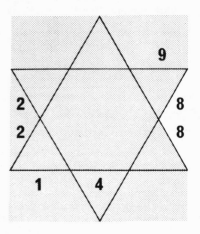

Strong reasoning powers are enjoyed by persons possessing this double number, but they must guard against projecting a dictatorial attitude toward others. They prefer to experience things for themselves, as they rarely believe other people's opinions, unless they have personally validated them. Double Eight persons also experience the need for constant change of surroundings, and it is of prime importance that they be given the opportunity to do so; otherwise severe frustrations could occur. These people should try to keep an open mind on subjects of a spiritual nature, realizing that standard, proven material laws do not apply in this area.

Three Eights (8 8 8) or More

Example: Date of Birth 8/18/1928

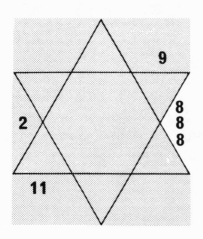

Example: Date of Birth 8/8/1898

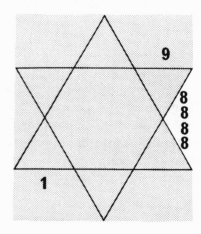

This is a very rare combination, that can, if people use it correctly, achieve dramatic results, provided their feet are firmly planted on the ground. Extreme restlessness is again apparent, so it is essential that this love of change and constant moving be experienced early in life, thus leaving middle and latter years to settle down to the tasks at hand. These people excel in the field of business and finance, as they are able accurately to assess most situations and use them to their advantage.

Frequent restrictions are placed on them, but they can usually be overcome with a positive attitude toward life. It is strange that, although they possess the ability to assess situations accurately, the inability to recognize opportunities is also very apparent. Although this is an extreme configuration, it is easier to handle than most, provided these people do not become too conscious of material possessions. They must realize that money and chattels alone rarely bring happiness or peace of mind.

ASPECTS FORMED BY THE NUMBER NINE

Single Nine (9)

Example: Date of Birth 5/6/1932

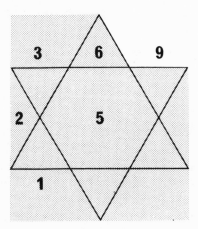

Obviously, everyone born within this century would possess at least one number Nine in his or her chart, so it holds no singular personal significance. But it is interesting to note that, as the number Nine appears on the mind and action lines, it comes as no surprise that, from the year 1900, man's accomplishments escalated at a tremendous rate. Discoveries and inventions that have derived from man's newfound knowledge and greater awareness of the mind are being put into use and action. Centuries ago, far-reaching individuals way ahead of their time conceived ideas similar to those of men and women now. Yet their ideas remained concepts, often being completely ridiculed by others around them.

The century we now live in allows creative people to utilize these concepts by *coupling* them with *action*. This century alone has produced more material accomplishments than any other similar period of time within man's known history. Needless to say, the single Nine holds a total significance of the desire to pursue mental activity to the full.

Two Nines (9 9)

Example: Date of Birth 3/19/1958

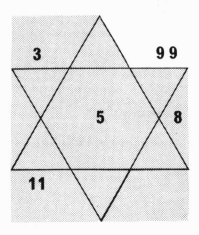

This combination signifies great mental ability, high level of intelligence, and the desire to question our very existence. Many philosophers and people of profound wisdom have been born with this double number configuration. Their deep thinking ability can be of tremendous benefit to mankind if used correctly. There are, however, a few character traits that cause problems for these people. Awareness of their mental ability often makes them short-tempered and critical of others who are unable to share this level of intelligence. They must realize that every man and woman possesses individual talents that are neither inferior nor superior to their own.

They should also mix freely with people from all walks of life. The tendency to work and socialize with their own kind often increases their air of superiority. Physical exercise must be included in their daily routine, as constant mental stimulation can lead to total exhaustion.

Three Nines (9 9 9) or More

Example: Date of Birth 9/9/1947

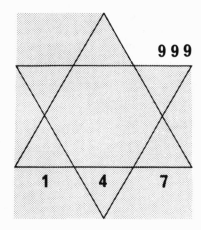

Example: Date of Birth 9/9/1939

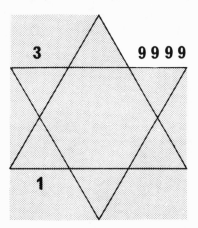

This triple configuration indicates tremendous activity of the mind that must be channeled into the right areas. The powerful mental ability of these persons can, if used correctly, be harmonious to their very existence. But if not used correctly, enormous mental frustrations can occur which could render them incapable of making logical day-to-day conclusions and decisions. As with the double Nine, these people must guard against feeling and appearing superior to others. Other people will naturally look up to and admire their mental prowess, but this must be recognized as an admiration of one talent alone and not of the person as a whole. Violent temper tantrums are common, due to the pent-up powerhouse of mental activity within them.

Interpretation of Full and Missing Number Lines Within the Natal Chart Full Number Lines

In the previous section we learned how to construct the natal chart and the interpretations of the various individual and multiple aspects that can occur. Now we will look at full and missing number lines to see how they can sharpen our degree of accuracy.

FULL NUMBER LINES

If we refer back to page 67, the areas within the double triangular configuration were divided into thought, will, action, mind, soul, and physical lines. We must now add two further full line combinations to this list, i.e., 1, 5, and 9 determination line, and the 3, 5, and 7 compassion line.

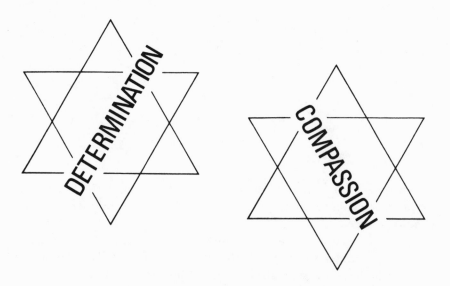

The addition of these two lines provides a total of eight possible full-line combinations. Below, we look at each individual line, together with its corresponding Numerological interpretation. As in the previous chapter, we have given illustrations of charts bearing these full-line combinations. The interpretation applies to the line in question only. The shaded areas within the chart should be ignored.

One, Two, and Three (1–2–3) Full Thought Line

Example: Date of Birth 9/2/1938

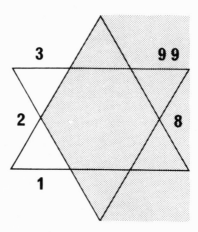

This denotes people who seek to live in an orderly, organized fashion. Tidiness is of prime importance to them, and they require it of others around them, but ironically they frequently are very untidy themselves. Consequently, misunderstandings and conflicts can occur when they fail to practice what they preach. Persons possessing this combination have the ability to plan vast business enterprises and effect efficient control. They must learn to consider and evaluate even the smallest of tasks as being important and essential to their final goal. This tendency frequently undermines their business expertise, but this can be overcome if they learn to delegate duties to those around them.

Basically, they are thoughtful people, but during times of pressure and crisis, they tend to overlook the needs of others. This happens because they are totally absorbed in their enterprises and schemes, thus leaving little time to consider the plight of others. However, when sadness and grief are brought to their attention, this same mind power is then redirected to seek an effective solution. Needless to say, a person possessing this combination could be a good friend in times of need, provided, first, that the problem is of some magnitude and, second, that they are made absolutely aware that it does exist.

Four, Five, and Six (4–5–6) Full Will Line

Example: Date of Birth 5/14/1936

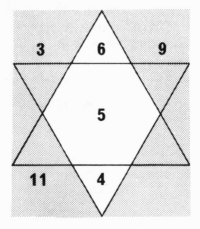

This signifies strong willpower, which if utilized for the good of the community and the needs of others can bring far-reaching rewards to those having this full will line. The number Six represents love of home, the Five, love of people, and the Four is associated with loyalty. Consequently, people possessing this combination usually experience a happy, balanced, and long-lasting friendship or marriage. The need to include others in their life is significant, as they naturally blend with people and are able to change their mood to suit any occasion with apparent ease. This need for involvement with others, together with their abundance of willpower, should be utilized fully within the areas of charity or social work.

Seven, Eight, and Nine (7–8–9) Full Action Line

Example: Date of Birth 8/17/1952

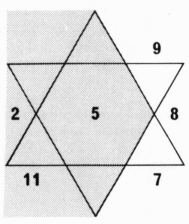

As you would expect, this signifies tremendous action. No sooner is the word spoken than the deed is done—a rare attribute these days. Those with the full action line should get plenty of outdoor exercise, eat the right foods, and above all get plenty of sleep. By doing this they are able to stabilize their great physical and mental abilities. But if this regimen isn't followed, then emotional disturbances could result.

It is essential that these people surround themselves with happy, stimulating company, avoiding situations or persons that are likely to bring disharmony and discord into their lives.

By coupling creative people with these action people, tremendous business achievements can be initiated, provided goals are clearly known and defined beforehand.

Three, Six, and Nine (3–6–9) Full Mind Line

Example: Date of Birth 6/13/1948

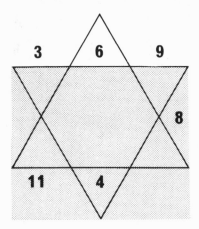

This indicates a well-balanced mind, capable of logical thought. A good memory is also enjoyed, as is a high degree of intelligence. These people must guard against becoming irritable with others who do not possess the same mind comprehension and intelligence as themselves. They shoulder home responsibilities adequately, as their balanced mind rationalizes and seeks out the logical answer to many of life's constant problems.

If these wonderful qualities can be directed toward the benefit of mankind, then purpose in life of those with the full mind line is realized and appreciated by all. But if these qualities are used solely for individual monetary gains, they could well find themselves very lonely people, seeking the same consolations that they have been unable to give themselves. It is an exceptional combination, and persons possessing it should dedicate themselves toward exploring and furthering their mental capacity.

Two, Five, and Eight (2–5–8) Full Soul Line

Example: Date of Birth 8/12/1957

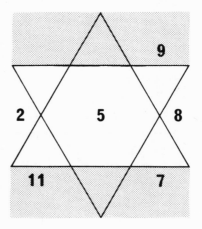

These open-minded people are able to adjust to all types of situations and circumstances. They are highly sensitive people who can use their senses to the fullest, being able to recognize another's happiness or sorrow in a flash. This intuitive awareness often attracts complete strangers to them, who unfold their whole life's problems and worries on their broad and strong shoulders. This ability to help and understand others can be fully appreciated within the areas of social help or welfare.

Unfortunately, although they are able to help so many others, they often experience extreme difficulties with their own problems. Their broad shoulders seem to sag noticeably under the weight of personal emotional troubles. However, other people invariably come to their aid. Repeated emotional disturbances can tend to lead those with this combination into a life of escapism, concerning themselves only with people in their own sphere and completely forgetting others on the outside. Luckily, it is rare to find persons with this line practicing this negative trait; usually it is a wonderful combination and those having it provide service well beyond the call of duty.

One, Four, and Seven (1–4–7) Full Physical Line

Example: Date of Birth 6/4/1937

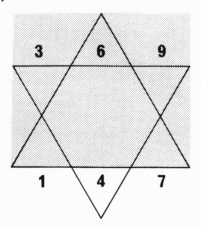

This line indicates healthy persons with excellent physical abilities and stamina. They excel in the fields of music, either from an appreciation point of view, or more usually from the ability of being able to master an instrument and reach a level of adequacy in a remarkably short time.

Beneath their brash exterior, there lie sensitive persons who abound in creative energy. But this energy must find a suitable outlet, otherwise they become frustrated and anxiety-stricken. Art and creative use of their hands can often provide this suitable release valve. They must guard against becoming too concerned with fleeting material values; they should rise above such things and seek to find themselves.

This is a powerful combination that can harbor tremendous talent, but frequently experiences restrictions and setbacks in life, as it combines influences of the numbers Four and Seven.

One, Five, and Nine (1–5–9) Full Determination Line

Example: Date of Birth 3/26/1945

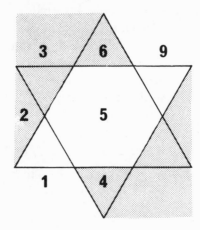

This indicates a spirit of determination and the ability to pursue tasks with dogged tenacity—wonderful traits to possess. Those possessing this line overcome obstacles within their path and eventually wear down restrictions until the way is open. Occasionally, temper tantrums and impatience will show through, but they only seem to strengthen their singular determination. They must learn to respect people they deal with on the way up life's ladder, as they will invariably need them again if they suffer reverses and find themselves on the way down. A well-adjusted person can be expected if this powerful force is used for the good of mankind. But if used destructively, then a hurtful person could eventuate.

Three, Five, and Seven (3–5–7) Full Compassion Line

Example: Date of Birth 5/13/1947

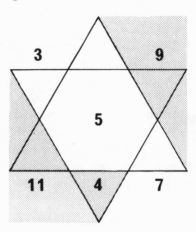

This is a wonderful line to possess, as it reflects great inner calm. These persons attract conditions of serenity and compassion which help them to understand the needs of others. They often have psychic powers coupled with a spiritual understanding far superior to any other full line.

Unfortunately, they often lead a life of sorrow, experiencing sad burdens and troubles throughout their years. Yet, it is this sadness that heightens their profound compassion for their fellowmen. The influence of the number Seven is great on this line, as it subdues and pacifies the outward gay abandon of the numbers Three and Five.

They are able to accept without question all of life's frequent hardships, and it is this factor that admirably equips them for their purpose in life—to help others. An unusual but highly desirable combination.

MISSING NUMBER LINES

It would be totally impossible for a person to have the single number 1 missing from his or her chart. Consequently, the one, two, and three (1–2–3) thought line, one, four, and seven (1–4–7) physical, and one, five, and nine (1–5–9) determination line can never be totally empty. It is also impossible, of course, for those born within this century to be missing the number Nine from their chart. This would then make the three, six, and nine (3–6–9) mind line and seven, eight, and nine (7–8–9) action lines incomplete. The remaining two, five, and eight (2–5–8) soul line, four, five, and six (4–5–6) will line, and three, five, and seven (3–5–7) compassion line are the only lines that can be totally empty within a natal chart.

For the interpretation of the part missing number lines, refer to the next section that deals with single missing numbers.

Two, Five, and Eight (2–5–8) Soul Line Missing

Example: Date of Birth 7/3/1961

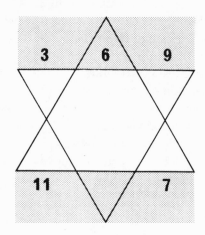

This indicates an early inferiority complex and the inability to mix and mingle with others. Lack of confidence and self-esteem are also evident in this missing configuration. However, these people have one consoling aspect: an ability to analyze accurately the character of a person on first impressions. The desire to escape from reality becomes apparent, as they often feel decidedly uncomfortable in the company of others. They should take every opportunity to become involved with people, because in doing so their introverted nature can be counter-balanced by bright, happy, stimulating associations.

Four, Five, and Six (4–5–6) Will Line Missing

Example: Date of Birth 3/17/1928

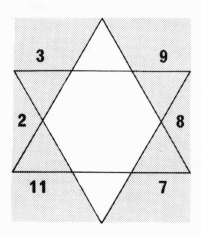

This is an unfortunate configuration, as it often indicates family or home separations. It can also point to a somewhat strained relationship or alienation from one or both parents during childhood. This frequently occurs through parents being overly protective or too dominant in their attitude, thus suppressing the child's independence and natural enthusiasm. People possessing this missing line generally suffer from lack of willpower and the inclination to give up a task at the first sign of opposition. Bearing this factor in mind, it comes as no surprise to find problems occurring in home and marriage, as they lack the desired tenacity and dedication so essential to a successful marriage or partnership. If they are able to realize this weakness and rectify it during early years, the chance of these problems occurring is greatly diminished.

They usually require somebody behind them in both home and business affairs, and it is of prime importance that people without these numbers in their chart associate with go-ahead, decision-making types, who can complement the above weaknesses.

Three, Five, and Seven (3–5–7) Compassion Line Missing

Example: Date of Birth 6/18/1942

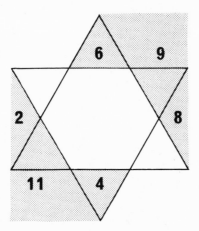

Often in Numerology and occult research analysis, we find aspects occurring in an individual's chart that apply to somebody else close to them. Such is the case here, as it would appear that somebody close to a person lacking this compassion line experiences nervous pain in the form of migraine headaches, eye and ear trouble.

Basically this aspect indicates a lack of spiritual awareness, with greater interest being placed upon the material aspects of life. It is important for these people to broaden their outlook on life and search more deeply from within, as here the answers to their frustrations and problems will be found.

SINGLE MISSING NUMBERS

Now that we have dealt with the three complete missing lines, we must now look at the single missing numbers within a natal chart. Referring back to the section that dealt with aspects formed by single, double, and triple or more numbers (derived from the date of birth), the reader can see how the traits generalized within the single number became more explicit, pronounced, or powerful as the combinations increased, i.e., One (1), two Ones (1 1), three Ones (1 1 1) or more. The combination of these aspects, together with the birth number interpretation and full and missing line analysis, does provide accurate results, but by including single missing number interpretations, the analysis can be humanized and rounded off to provide a complete individual character reading.

The interpretations given below indicate negative or weak characteristics for each possible missing number.

Number One (1)

It is impossible for persons to be missing this number from their chart.

Number Two (2)

This indicates lack of sensitivity and intuition, which can often result in the wrong choice of partners, both in the home and the business. These people must learn to consider the little things of life, as they often lack the desire or ability to pay attention to detail.

Patience is not one of their virtues, which seems strange as they are noted for being extremely unpunctual. Obviously, they expect other people to be patient, when they themselves are not.

Number Three (3)

Lack of loyalty, confidence, self-esteem, and the inability to express oneself are shown here. Threes must learn not to underestimate their ability or sell themselves short in life. Recognition of artistic beauty is diminished greatly with the exclusion of this number. The normal, bright, happy, artistic definition of the number Three can be replaced by a drab, nondemonstrative individual. If they are able to realize this basic weakness early in life and dedicate themselves toward dramatic self-expression, then the negative trait of this missing number can generally be overcome.

Number Four (4)

This indicates lack of routine, order, and system. Consequently, persons lacking this number often lead lives of total confusion, unable to realize that, by applying simple organizational techniques, their weaknesses can be overcome and life can be more effective and beneficial. They are not usually fond of work and have to be pushed and goaded to produce results. The general ability of the hands, associated with this number, is not enjoyed here. Their hardships and limitations are self-inflicted, and realization of this simple fact can often change their lives overnight.

Number Five (5)

This missing number is very common, and it clearly indicates lack of drive, adaptability, and versatility in life. These persons constantly need a push from others, and this desire to be motivated, rather than to motivate others usually follows them through life. They are not determined people and find it extremely hard to set goals let alone follow them through to the end. They must learn to consider the emotions and feelings of their fellowmen and realize that they, more than any other person, require the help and guidance of others around them.

Number Six (6)

This often shows lack of a stable family background with problems and difficulties during childhood. These home complications usually occur as a result of difficulties with the father rather than the mother. Those missing number Six must realize that associations and partnerships between two people do not just happen, and that each person must be prepared to give more than he or she takes. They must also learn to express their emotions outwardly, as they tend to overlook or suppress their innermost feelings, especially concerning family matters. Problems surrounding home and marriage frequently follow these people through life. But like all negative traits, these can be overcome if they realize their weaknesses and try wherever possible to consider others foremost in their relationships.

Number Seven (7)

This signifies lack of spiritual expression and nonacceptance of metaphysical facts. It also shows a somewhat disorganized approach to life, a seeking to stumble from day to day rather than planning for the future. A missing Seven also indicates that in these people there is a tendency to be inconsiderate of other people's opinions and feelings. They desire to ignore advice and prefer to make their own decisions regardless of conflicting circumstances. They must give attention to health, diet, and nonabuse of the body, as their natural physical resistance is not strong.

Number Eight (8)

This shows lack of business efficiency and financial ability. It is common to find individuals with an Eight missing from their natal chart to be both careless with money and illogical in their judgment of same. It is essential that these people appoint an accountant or qualified individual to handle their financial affairs, especially if they are self-employed or in a position of authority.

Those who are missing this number seldom finish tasks and continually leave loose ends untied. High points in life must be consolidated, otherwise material rewards could well be lost very quickly. Reliance on other people is common, due to the fact that the missing Eight lacks self-confidence and is afraid to tackle tasks independently. These people need constant motivation, as the tendency to become lazy is very apparent.

Number Nine (9)

Obviously persons born in this century possess a number Nine in their natal chart. However, for those born prior to the twentieth century and for those who will invariably enter this world in the twenty-first century, the following applies: Lack of humanitarianism and the ability to understand the needs and desires of others. There is a basic fear of expressing their emotions, as they consider this a weak character trait. They prefer not to become involved with individuals and their problems, choosing to isolate themselves and their emotions.

They should learn to cultivate a need for other people, realizing that, like themselves, others also require sympathy and understanding. The failure to accept the mental abilities and capabilities of others is clearly shown, with the result that they frequently underestimate their opposition.

6

The Rhythm of the Universe

Universal Years, Months, and Days

Each single year produces a rhythm and vibration that have a significant bearing on the world and people within it. Throughout history, the progression of years and also single years have proved to be highly significant, often changing man's path throughout life. Therefore, it is essential that we now learn the universal year cycles and the various vibrations that they impart on us.

Calculation of the Universal Year Numbers

To calculate the universal year numbers is very simple. We merely take the year in question and add the single digits together, to produce either a single number of 1 to 9, or a master number of 11 or 22. Let's look at some examples:

Example 1
> To find the universal year number for the year 1939:
> Add together *individually* all the digits of the year 1939:
> > $1 + 9 + 3 + 9 = 22.$

The universal year number for 1939 is 22.

Example 2
> To find the universal year number for the year 1963:
> Add together individually all the digits of the year 1963:
> > $1 + 9 + 6 + 3 = 19 = 10 = 1$

The universal year number for 1963 is 1.

Example 3

To find the universal year number for the year 1982:

Add together individually all the digits of the year 1982:

$$1 + 9 + 8 + 2 = 20 = 2$$

The universal year number for the year 1982 is 2.

Universal years do not apply directly to individuals, but rather to the community and the world as a whole.

We have given the following brief descriptions of trends likely to be experienced during each universal year.

Interpretations of the Universal Year Vibrations

One (1) Universal Year

New beginnings, inventions. General optimistic attitude and a striving toward new frontiers.

Two (2) Universal Year

Peaceful coexistence. Consolidation of efforts and people.

Three (3) Universal Year

Inspired happiness. Vision. Dreams and fulfillment.

Four (4) Universal Year

Organization of country and world affairs. Hard working conditions.

Five (5) Universal Year

Joining of people. New formations and associations. Renewed vigor.

Six (6) Universal Year

Harmony of world conditions. Protection of and help given to underprivileged countries.

Seven (7) Universal Year

Consolidation and perfection. Agriculture and ecological pursuits heightened.

Eight (8) Universal Year

Expansion and material gain. Increase in general prosperity.

Nine (9) Universal Year
Love and fulfillment. World peace and harmony consolidated.

Eleven (11) Universal Year
Spiritual gains. Questioning of present ideals. Increase of religious pursuits.

Twenty-two (22) Universal Year
Worldly expansion. Greater emphasis and awareness placed on peaceful coexistence.

When calculating universal and cycles of universal years, it will be found that the general progression follows from 1 through to 9. However, certain years have master vibrations with the result that the sequence can take the form of:

    a. 1 (11), 3, 4, 5, 6, 7, 8, 9, and
    b. 1, 2, 3 (22), 5, 6, 7, 8, 9

As we have stated many times, Numerology defines the progression and sequences that can occur throughout an individual's life. This same progression can apply on a universal basis. So let's now look at the interpretations of these nine-year cycles to see how Numerology defines a logical formation.

Remember that these universal yearly interpretations refer to the likely positive influences and not the negative ones. Obviously, men and nations are not totally positive. Therefore, the negative vibrations that could occur would represent complete opposites to those given. A negative Nine universal year could produce world conflict and aggression, as opposed to world peace and harmony.

Sequence of Universal Year Vibrations

Universal Year One (1)
Man commences a new cycle, looking toward developments of the future as a result of conditions of the past.

Universal Year Two (2)
He now starts to consolidate his aims and ambitions, endeavoring to create a peaceful and harmonious existence.

Universal Year Three (3)

From consolidation, he now projects thoughts and desires outwardly, utilizing creative inspirational peaks to accomplish his destiny.

Universal Year Four (4)

Man's inspirational activities must now be planned and brought down to earth, ready for practical application.

Universal Year Five (5)

Man's inward practicality ceases and he can now outwardly express and activate his schemes and desires. He realizes that all worldly concepts relate directly to people; therefore they must be considered before all else.

Universal Year Six (6)

Man now realizes the full implications and necessity of building a future world based on stable education of the young, together with development of the underprivileged.

Universal Year Seven (7)

Man's grandiose humanitarian schemes must now be planned and perfected. His desire to help the underprivileged now becomes reality by development within the areas of agriculture and farming.

Universal Year Eight (8)

Nature, together with the laws of life, now rewards man for his concern for others. He experiences greater prosperity, which in turn can be used for the good of the community.

Universal Year Nine (9)

Man's nine-year cycle is now finishing. Past plans and schemes have been completed and much knowledge has been gained, providing a firm basis to embark on a new nine-year cycle of life.

We will now look at the master 11 and 22 universal years to see how they affect the previous cycle.

Universal Year Eleven (11)

Following man's thoughts for a new beginning, he now questions material worldly ideals and seeks greater spiritual fulfillment. He sadly realizes that schemes and concepts of a far-reaching humanitarian nature must be rearranged to suit a somewhat idealistic community.

Universal Year Twenty-two (22)

Following the joyous outward expression and happiness of the last three years, man experiences deep guilt feelings toward the plight of others. Consequently, vast humanitarian schemes and enterprises are inaugurated to improve world conditions. Nature has awakened man to his responsibilities and moral obligations.

Calculation of Universal Month Numbers

To calculate the universal month number in any given year, we must add all the digits of the month to the year in question, to produce either a single number of 1 to 9, or the master numbers of 11, 22, or 33.

Example 1

To find the universal month number for July 1940:

Step a. Calendar month number for July = 7

Step b. Now add the number 7 to the individual digits of the year 1940:

$$7 + 1 + 9 + 4 + 0 = 21 = 3$$

The universal month number for July 1940 is 3.

Example 2

To find the universal month number for April 1958:

Step a. Calendar month number for April = 4

Step b. Add the number 4 to the individual digits of the year 1958:

$$4 + 1 + 9 + 5 + 8 = 27 = 9$$

The universal month number for April 1958 is 9.

Example 3

To find the universal month number for January 1983:

Step a. Calendar month number for January = 1

Step b. Add the number 1 to the individual digits of the year 1983:

$$1 + 1 + 9 + 8 + 3 = 22$$

The universal month number for January 1983 is 22.

For interpretations of the universal months, refer to the meanings given for each universal year and apply them in reference to a single month, rather than for a twelve-month period.

The universal year interpretations omitted the master 33 number, as there will be no master 33 universal year until 6999. However, it is possible to currently have a 33 universal month, so the following interpretation should apply:

Universal Month Thirty-Three (33)

The harmony of world conditions as shown in the vibration of Six would be greatly intensified, as would the steps taken toward helping underprivileged countries and individuals. This extreme vibration could lead to extraordinary decisions and schemes being implemented.

From the calculation of universal years and months, we must now progress even further to include the universal day.

Calculation of Universal Day Numbers

The calculation of the universal day number is very simple, as it is basically identical to the steps taken to arrive at an individual's life path number; i.e., all the digits of the month, day, and year in question are added together individually, reducing to either a single digit of 1 to 9 or the three master numbers of 11, 22, and 33.

Let's look at two examples:

Example 1

To find the universal day number for November 12, 1960:

Step a. Reduce the full date to numbers:

11/12/1960

Step b. Add all the digits of the date together individually:

$1 + 1 + 1 + 2 + 1 + 9 + 6 + 0 = 21$

Step c. Add the remaining two digits together:

$2 + 1 = 3$

The universal day number for November 12, 1960, is 3.

Example 2

To find the universal day number for September 24, 1922:

Step a. Reduce the full date to numbers:

9/24/1922

Step b. Add all the digits of the date together individually:

$$9 + 2 + 4 + 1 + 9 + 2 + 2 = 29$$

Step c. Add the remaining two digits together:

$$2 + 9 = 11$$

The universal day number for September 24, 1922, is 11.

Note: For information relating to zeros and master numbers, refer to the calculations of life path numbers, as the method is identical.

The significance and meanings of the universal day number vibrations can be gained by utilizing the universal year interpretations and relating them to a single day, as opposed to one year.

As we stated previously, the universal year, month, and day number vibrations hold a significance that relates to the world in general. It is essential to know how to calculate and interpret these universal numbers, as this knowledge can provide a firm basis to understanding world trends at any given time. The next chapter will deal with personal year, month, and day numbers, which will hold far greater individual significance. However, we will explain later how these universal vibrations can be used in conjunction with the individual vibrations and birth numbers to produce an instant guide to harmony.

7

What Kind of Year, Month, or Day?

Personal Year, Month, and Day Numbers

In the previous chapter we explained how to calculate years, months, and days. Now we will see how Numerology can provide a wealth of individual guidance by calculating the personal year, month, and day vibrations. Knowledge of these vibrations can provide a sound basis for planning new enterprises and concepts or making important decisions at a time when we are at harmony with our very being.

Calculation of Personal Year Numbers

To calculate any personal year number, we merely add an individual's month and day of birth to the year in question.

Example 1

To find the personal year number for an individual born on September 12, 1932, during the year 1977:

Step a. Take the day and month of birth, together with the year in question:
9/12/1977

Step b. Add all the digits together *individually*:
$9 + 1 + 2 + 1 + 9 + 7 + 7 = 36$

Step c. Add the remaining two digits together:
$3 + 6 = 9$

The personal year number for an individual born on September 12, 1932, during the year 1977 is 9.

Note: This method is identical to the one used for the calculation of the life path number, the only difference being that of substituting the year in question for the individual's year of birth. For references relating to zero and master numbers, refer back to the life path calculation and examples, as the necessary steps also apply here.

To strengthen our understanding of this calculation, let's look at some further examples.

Example 2

To find the personal year number for an individual born on August 10, 1927, during the year 1970:

Step a. Take the day and month of birth, together with the year in question:

8/10/1970

Step b. Add all the digits together individually:

$8 + 1 + 0 + 1 + 9 + 7 + 0 = 26$

Step c. Add the remaining two digits together:

$2 + 6 = 8$

The personal year number for an individual born on August 10, 1927, during the year 1970 is 8.

Example 3

To find the personal year number for an individual born on July 19, 1943, during the year 1974:

Step a. Take the day and month of birth, together with the year in question:

7/19/1974

Step b. Add all the digits together individually:

$7 + 1 + 9 + 1 + 9 + 7 + 4 = 38$

Step c. Add the remaining two digits together:

$3 + 8 = 11$

Do not reduce further as 11 is a master number.

The personal year number for an individual born on July 19, 1943, during the year 1974 is 11.

Example 4

To find the personal year number for an individual born on March 1, 1928, during the year 1980:

Step a. Take the day and month of birth, together with the year in question:

3/1/1980

Step b. Add all the digits together individually:

$3 + 1 + 1 + 9 + 8 + 0 = 22$

Do not reduce further as 22 is a master number.

The personal year number for an individual born on March 1, 1928, during the year 1980 is 22.

These calculations can apply to past, present, and future, providing a valuable template for personal vibrations, their cause and effect.

Personal year vibrations are extremely important; they apply to each one of us individually and change from year to year. It is as essential to recognize and take advantage of the exceptional vibrations as it is being aware of and endeavoring to reduce the effects of the detrimental vibrations.

The next section deals with each personal year number, indicating what can be expected throughout that twelve-month period. It also offers advice to show how these vibrations can be used to their fullest individual advantage.

Interpretation and Significance of Personal Year Vibrations

A One (1) Personal Year

Physical strength is now at its highest peak, making it a perfect time to initiate new schemes, concepts, and adventures. Life will now take on a new challenge, and since those with this number will be physically able to cope with it makes it an enjoyable time. Goals should be clearly set and worked toward, as this is a commencing cycle and the future should hold greater significance than the past. Problems and disappointments experienced in the previous years will now disappear, leaving the way open to a wonderful new way of life. This is a powerful, personal year that should *always* be used to its fullest advantage.

A Two (2) Personal Year

This is a year for accumulation and consolidation. It affords a much-needed breathing space between the hectic One and Three years. The previous year's ambitions and challenges should now be looked at and analyzed for their practical success and value, for now is the time to streamline, change, and perfect schemes for the future. New ideas and innovations will come as a direct result of mixing with other people, for this is indeed a year of togetherness.

As opposed to the One year, when individual pursuits left little time for other people, this is a year of group achievement, when sharing experiences with others is essential. Patience should be exercised this year, as startling, heart-stopping opportunities and decisions will not arise, but behind-the-scenes action is gaining momentum. Take a breather, mix and mingle, and enjoy the company of others, for now is the time to recharge the batteries for the next hectic year ahead.

A Three (3) Personal Year

This is a year to look forward to, as it exudes happy and bright vibrations. Life should now be lived to the full. Socialize, accept new invitations, and take full advantage of a lessening of responsibilities. This is a wonderfully happy year for outward expression and activities, but it can be a disastrous year on the business scene. The happy, frivolous atmosphere that now exists could well infiltrate into business areas, causing rash decisions and impractical, unfinished schemes.

However, life is so full on the social scene that little time is left for exhausting business efforts. *Joie de vivre* is a wonderful attitude to possess, but unfortunately it diminishes the bank balance dramatically. However, the next year will quickly rectify this problem.

A Four (4) Personal Year

The previous year's frivolity will now be well and truly forgotten, as the facts of life are clearly spelled out. This is a year of hard work and effort when one must knuckle down to the task at hand. It is a frustrating year when considerable effort rarely produces dramatic results. One step forward and two steps back seems to be the motto of this year. Past failures and successes must now be carefully examined, as this is an organizational period designed to bring a person down to earth. Responsibilities will increase, thus magnifying the effort and hard work needed to maintain a reasonable level of existence. Health and diet should be carefully scrutinized during this year, as physical resistance is low, increasing susceptibility to ailments. Tidying up of affairs is now in order, as one must make ready for a very hectic year ahead.

A Five (5) Personal Year

This is a year to look forward to and enjoy, as the previous twelve months of hard physical effort have ended. Anything can be tackled now, provided the governing overtones of restlessness can be somewhat subdued. Travel, holidays, change, and variety will all be enjoyed during this hectic, fun-loving year. Mundane daily routine that was previously tackled by necessity will now be recharged with physical electricity.

Throwing out the old and welcoming the new should be the motto for this year, as it heralds a new positive approach to life. One must beware of clandestine relationships that could endanger existing security. A tendency to throw all to the wind will prevail. Balance is an essential factor to maintain during this period, otherwise the dominant theme of the next year could be disastrous.

A Six (6) Personal Year

Romance, love, and home are of paramount importance during this twelve-month period. The gay, abandoned, carefree existence of the preceding year is now brought down to earth by the realization and greater awareness of security and responsibility. This is a year in which the patter of tiny feet or, rather, the ear-piercing cry of a newborn baby could reverberate through the house. Nature reigns supreme in conditioning and preparing for parenthood, and Numerology works hand in hand with nature when a person is in a Six personal year.

Nothing of a startling nature occurs outside the home, as occupations and professions tend to take on a new dimension, becoming secondary to home affairs. The burning drive and ambition of the previous year are now replaced with a realization that the end result is purely a material entity, as opposed to love of family and home which has no bearing whatsoever on financial esteem. The new company that this year brings must be enjoyed to the full, as again nature steps in to test strength of character within the next twelve months.

A Seven (7) Personal Year

This is a somewhat lonely year, when one seeks to look from within for the answers to life rather than sharing problems with others. Spiritual learning and fulfillment are heightened during this period, when the joys of the previous twelve months are now being weighed against the realities of life. Priorities are now questioned and new conclusions reached, often vastly different from previous standards. This is a waiting year when one must be prepared to consolidate and mark time, exercising extreme patience.

Future ventures should now be carefully examined, analyzed, and streamlined to fulfill ambitions in life. This personal year can rightly be thought of as the lull before the storm, and good use must be made of this somewhat quiet period to strengthen and fortify the constitution to be ready for the powerful year ahead.

An Eight (8) Personal Year

This is an extremely powerful year when innermost dreams and ambitions can be fulfilled. Thoughts and concepts can be put into action. The physical body is now at a peak, primed by nature to tackle any task. Now is the time for action, and there should be no need to procrastinate or think unduly about any new venture.

Provided the seeds of fulfillment have been carefully planted in the preceding seven years, rewards will eventuate at a pace far greater than originally expected. Consequently, it is of prime importance to be prepared for speedy results, learning to utilize the rewards accordingly. Personal ambition, which is the driving force during this year, is again questioned by nature within the next twelve-month cycle.

A Nine (9) Personal Year

This is a stocktaking year, when previous values, ideals, and influences should be carefully scrutinized. As opposed to the previous year, this is a period when giving to others holds far greater significance than looking out for oneself. Home environment, relationships, and associations are important now, as becomes the awareness and appreciation of the finer free benefits in life. There is also the desire to commune with nature, away from the hustle and bustle of big-city life. This is a consolidation year when debts, schemes, and plans must be finished and cleared from the mind, to make ready for a new nine-year life cycle.

An Eleven (11) Personal Year

The vibrations of this personal year are primarily concerned with spiritual ideals rather than material gains or possessions. It is a time when the light at the end of the tunnel begins to glow brighter, bringing new meanings and depth to life. Provided the correct perspective is taken, wonderful, far-reaching rewards can be expected. Other people will be motivated and enlightened in the presence of persons in this personal year, as the signpost of life is clearly pointing in their direction. As it is an extremely personal year, some emotional difficulties can be expected. This usually comes as a direct result of the desire to question present ideals, circumstances, and situations.

A Twenty-two (22) Personal Year

This is a year to remember, as restrictions will now be lifted and the way will be open to plan and instigate far-reaching, all-inspiring aims and ambitions. There will be absolutely no limit to what can be achieved during these twelve months, as the seeds that have been planted in previous years will now begin to break through the earth and stretch up to the sun. This is the master year and to misuse it would be a great loss.

Both physical and mental activity are now at a peak, and the body is suitably conditioned to accommodate the work and effort involved in initiating grandiose schemes. To realize the full benefit from this wonderful year, efforts toward the community or fellowmen hold far greater significance than personal material gains. It is essential that schemes begun during this year be fully carried through, as the current power and effectiveness will only last for a twelve-month period.

A Thirty-three (33) Personal Year

This is a year when home conditions will completely dominate life's activities. The general interpretation of a Six personal year does apply here, but with emphasis on extreme conditions existing. Affairs of the heart will be highlighted during this period of life, and caution must be taken against going overboard with any romantic associations. There is a tendency to forget responsibilities in favor of a new, more exciting relationship. Physical awareness and desires now manifest themselves, often creating frustration through lack of fulfillment. Prior responsibilities now act as a mental prison, suppressing personal individuality.

Wide-open spaces and love of the natural life will now be sought after, and if possible frequent trips to the country should be taken, as this would provide a natural release valve for the frustrations and mental complications now being experienced.

Calculation of Personal Month Numbers

Now that we have mastered the art of personal year numbers, we must move on to the calculations of the personal months. There are many different methods that can be utilized, but the method given below has proved to be the easiest. The personal month calculation is simply the logical progression of adding the calendar month number to the personal year number. As always, the final answer should reduce to the single numbers of 1 to 9 or the master numbers of 11, 22, and 33. The three master numbers should *not* be reduced. Here are several examples.

Example 1

If we wish to calculate the personal month number of July 1946 for a person born on 9/12/1928, we must take the following three steps:

Step a. Repeat the first part of the method given for the calculation of the personal year number:

9/12/1928 now becomes 9/12/1946 (year in question)

Step b. Now add the calendar month number to this date:

9/12/1946 + 7 (calendar month number for July)

Step c. Add all the digits of the year and month together individually:

9 + 1 + 2 + 1 + 9 + 4 + 6 + 7 = 39 = 12 = 3

The personal month number of July 1946 for a person born on 9/12/1928 is 3.

Example 2

To calculate the personal month number of June 1982 for a person born on 11/13/1948:

Step a. Repeat the first part of the method given for the calculation of the personal year number:

11/13/1948 now becomes 11/13/1982 (year in question)

Step b. Add the calendar month number to this date:

11/13/1982 + 6 (calendar month for June)

Step c. Add all the digits of the year and month number together individually:

1 + 1 + 1 + 3 + 1 + 9 + 8 + 2 + 6 = 32 = 5

The personal month number of June 1982 for a person born on 11/13/1948 is 5.

Example 3

To calculate the personal month number of November 1977 for a person born on 9/12/1950:

Step a. Repeat the first part of the method given for the calculation of the personal year number:

9/12/1950 now becomes 9/12/1977 (year in question)

Step b. Add the calendar month number to this date:

9/12/1977 + 11 (calendar month number for November)

Step c. Add all the digits of the year and month together individually:

9 + 1 + 2 + 1 + 9 + 7 + 7 + 1 + 1 = 38 = 11

The personal month number of November 1977 for a person born on 9/12/1950 is 11.

The above examples should clearly illustrate the steps that must be taken to calculate any personal month number. As with the universal month numbers, it is unnecessary to provide lengthy explanations regarding the vibrations of each of these numbers. By utilizing interpretations given of the personal years and relating them to the months accurate results can be achieved.

This now leaves one final calculation, that being the addition of the personal day number.

Calculation of Personal Day Numbers

The method used to calculate the personal day number is identical to the sequence used for the year and month, but with the addition of one further step—that of including the day in question. Examples given below will clearly illustrate the steps needed to calculate any personal day number. It will be noticed that the first three steps are a repetition of the method needed to calculate the personal month number, but we have repeated these steps to provide practice and familiarization while learning.

Example 1

If we wish to calculate the personal day number of 8/13/1977 for a person born on 7/18/1960, we must take the following four steps:

Step a. Repeat the first part of the method given for the calculation of the personal year number:

7/18/1960 now becomes 7/18/1977 (year in question)

Step b. Add the calendar month number to this date:

7/18/1977 + 8 (calendar month number for August)

Step c. Add the calendar day to this date:

7/18/1977 + 8 + 13 (13th day)

Step d. Add all the digits of these year, month, and day numbers together individually:

$7 + 1 + 8 + 1 + 9 + 7 + 7 + 8 + 1 + 3 = 52 = 7.$

The personal day number of 8/13/1977 for a person born on 7/18/1960 is 7.

Example 2

To calculate the personal day number of 2/28/1986 for a person born on 11/6/1940:

Step a. Repeat the first part of the method given for the calculation of the personal year number:

11/6/1940 now becomes 11/6/1986 (year in question)

Step b. Add the calendar month number to this date:

11/6/1986 + 2 (calendar month number for February)

Step c. Add the calendar day to this date:

11/6/1986 + 2 + 28 (28th day)

Step d. Add all the digits of these year, month, and day numbers together individually:

$1 + 1 + 6 + 1 + 9 + 8 + 6 + 2 + 2 + 8 = 44 = 8$

The personal day number of 2/28/1986 for a person born on 11/6/1940 is 8.

Example 3

To calculate the personal day number of 10/11/1968 for a person born on 11/6/1928:

Step a. Repeat the first part of the method given for the calculation of the personal year number:

11/6/1928 now becomes 11/6/1968 (year in question)

Step b. Add the calendar month number to this date:

11/6/1968 + 10 (calendar month number for October)

Step c. Add the calendar day to this date:

11/6/1968 + 10 + 11 (11th day)

Step d. Add all the digits of these year, month, and day numbers together individually:

$1 + 1 + 6 + 1 + 9 + 6 + 8 + 1 + 0 + 1 + 1 = 35 = 8$

The personal day number of 10/11/1968 for a person born on 11/6/1928 is 8.

As when calculating the personal month numbers, attention should be given when reducing to the single and master numbers of 1 to 9 and 11, 22, and 33.

For interpretations relating to the personal day number vibrations, utilize personal year explanations and define them for a period of one day rather than one year.

We do suggest that the chapters dealing with universal and personal year, month, and day numbers be read very carefully and that the steps shown be followed as given. In time, you will no doubt streamline this method to provide a speedier end result, but it is of prime importance that before you attempt to do so, the simple but somewhat laborious method shown should be fully understood. It is easy to overlook one or more steps, and as you now realize, accuracy is utterly essential to the science of Numerology.

8

The Important Years

Divide your age in half and try to remember back to your outlook toward life as it was then. Was it identical to your feelings and thoughts now? In most cases the answer would be no, as it is totally natural for attitudes and outlooks to change as maturity increases. The child cannot understand the attitude or reasoning of the parent, until he or she becomes a parent. Parents cannot understand the attitude of their grandparents, until they also become grandparents. Such is the cycle of life.

Each day of our lives we experience new physical, emotional, and mental circumstances that seek to increase our level of awareness and understanding of life. We ride on the crest of a wave through life's highs and endeavor to scramble unscathed through life's low periods. Some years will always stand out as being worthy of remembrance and others, due to their unhappy memories, are best forgotten.

Experience can never be taught; only the knowledge gained from it can be passed on for the benefit of others. Experience is living, making mistakes, overcoming obstacles, conquering adversities. Yes, experience is indeed living and by living, experience can and will be gained.

Numerology has always placed great emphasis on experience, as its basic indoctrination that life should be spent learning and helping others can only be based on the profound realization of the importance of experience itself. Man experiences four major steps in life, until he reaches total mental awareness and maturity. A pyramid is used to illustrate these steps or phases of life—hence we refer to them as the pyramid years.

The Four Significant Steps

Step 1

From childhood to the first significant pyramid year, man's awareness of life is beginning to awaken. Personalities, individualities, likes

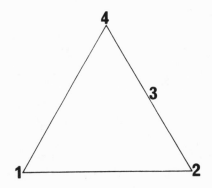

and dislikes are now being formulated and molded from within, to provide the basis for future years.

Step 2

Maturity increases and man now begins to realize his purpose in life. Responsibilities increase and a stabilizing of attitudes and actions now takes effect. This can be a somewhat troubled period, when man tends to be torn between the carefree memories of youth and the realization of the future.

Step 3

Man now progresses into the third stage of life. Physical/mental pressures and responsibilities now peak at a time when he is experiencing a reduction of effective ability. This is a trying period when impending age threatens his very being. The generation gap is now experienced and its realities are found hard to accept. Man's awareness and maturity have obviously increased, but physical capabilities are reduced, thus creating an imbalance. Offspring are growing older, but man is also aging at a seemingly faster rate.

Step 4

As man passes from the third to the fourth stage of life, his understanding reaches full and total significance. He no longer fights either to regain his youth or to evade his impending old age. Worldly material and spiritual values are now placed in their true proportion. Experience has produced knowledge.

The pyramid years of life differ with each life path number. The table illustrates the pyramid progressions for each life path number.

Table of Pyramid Years for Each Life Path Number

P/Y = PYRAMID YEARS

1.	1st P/Y	Positive	Negative	Positive	2nd P/Y	Positive	Negative	Positive	3rd P/Y	Positive	Negative	Positive	4th P/Y
1.	26	27 28	29 30 31	32 33 34	35	36 37	38 39 40	41 42 43	44	45 46	47 48 49	50 51 52	53
2.	16	17 18	19 20 21	22 23 24	25	26 27	28 29 30	31 32 33	34	35 36	37 38 39	40 41 42	43
3.	33	34 35	36 37 38	39 40 41	42	43 44	45 46 47	48 49 50	51	52 53	54 55 56	57 58 59	60
4.	32	33 34	35 36 37	38 39 40	41	42 43	44 45 46	47 48 49	50	51 52	53 54 55	56 57 58	59
5.	31	32 33	34 35 36	37 38 39	40	41 42	43 44 45	46 47 48	49	50 51	52 53 54	55 56 57	58
6.	30	31 32	33 34 35	36 37 38	39	40 41	42 43 44	45 46 47	48	49 50	51 52 53	54 55 56	57
7.	29	30 31	32 33 34	35 36 37	38	39 40	41 42 43	44 45 46	47	48 49	50 51 52	53 54 55	56
8.	28	29 30	31 32 33	34 35 36	37	38 39	40 41 42	43 44 45	46	47 48	49 50 51	52 53 54	55
9.	27	28 29	30 31 32	33 34 35	36	37 38	39 40 41	42 43 44	45	46 47	48 49 50	51 52 53	54
11.	25	26 27	28 29 30	31 32 33	34	35 36	37 38 39	40 41 42	43	44 45	46 47 48	49 50 51	52
22.	14	15 16	17 18 19	20 21 22	23	24 25	26 27 28	29 30 31	32	33 34	35 36 37	38 39 40	41
33.	30	31 32	33 34 35	36 37 38	39	40 41	42 43 44	45 46 47	48	49 50	51 52 53	54 55 56	57

Note: Years shown within this table represent actual ages for each life path number.

These ages should prove to be very significant for people throughout their lives, as decisions, experiences, and resolutions of a momentous nature are likely to occur within these years. Remember, these significant experiences can either be of positive or negative vibrations and influences.

You will notice that each phase of life between the pyramid years covers a nine-year span and that this in turn is divided into three three-year periods. Each phase heralds a new beginning that commences prior to the year in question, builds up to a crescendo during that year, and then wanes, slowly reducing in power after the pyramid year. Therefore, a period exists in between each new beginning; this is classed as a negative phase of life and lasts for a period of three years.

9

Putting It All Together

Complete Natal Chart Analysis

THE FIRST STEP

To date, we have dealt with each calculation relevant to the compilation of the natal chart. We are now in a position to combine all these factors to form one complete, concise, accurate analysis. Let's recap our knowledge so far.

First, we learned how to calculate the life path number, together with the placement into the double triangle of the individual digits gained from the date of birth. We utilized these aspects to form individual assessments relative to strengths and weaknesses. The birth day number was then taken into consideration, together with its significance. We saw how full and missing number lines added strength or created weakness to the individual chart, and how missing number interpretations were used to individualize and round off the analysis.

We must now combine all these calculations for the final analysis. This is best illustrated by looking at an example.

Example

To provide a complete natal chart resume for an individual born on November 12, 1931, we take the following steps:

Step 1. Calculate the life path number:

$$11/12/1931 = 1 + 1 + 1 + 2 + 1 + 9 + 3 + 1$$
$$= 19 = 10 = 1$$

The life number for this individual is 1.

Step 2. Compile the natal chart:

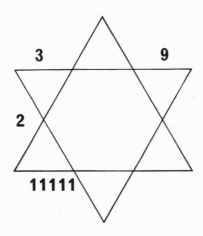

Step 3. Interpret the individual aspects shown within the chart.

We will deal with each aspect step by step, including the full interpretation applying to each individual sequence as it occurs.

WHAT THE NATAL CHART ANALYSIS INDICATES

Five Ones (1 1 1 1 1)

This clearly indicates an overtaxing of physical and mental energy. This type of person finds it extremely difficult to relax and turn off. They are constantly pushing themselves on both the mental and physical plane. Speech expression is extremely strong, to the extent of being overbearing in discussions and differences of opinion. The combination of five Ones or more can indicate an overly physical person, with strong basic desires and possibly leaning toward violence. This extreme combination of Ones can also point to obesity, overindulgence, and the desire to eat the wrong types of food.

This is a very strong aspect that needs a creative outlet for this pent-up energy. If an outlet is found, a happy, powerful, alert, and successful person would eventuate. But if a suitable outlet cannot be found, then a self-centered, moody, aggressive individual could result. From our experience, we have found many people with this strong combination of four or more Ones to be inwardly powerful but outwardly confused.

The literary and artistic fields provide ideal outlets for this pent-up energy. Generally, these people throw themselves into any task with enormous vigor and determination, thus often achieving dramatic results in an amazingly short space of time.

One Two (2)

Those who possess this single number have the ability to detect insincerity in others immediately, which usually results in them forming firm opinions on people at first meeting—luckily these opinions are rarely wrong. They are sensitive and intuitive people, but this sensitivity often makes them prone to emotional hardships. They must learn to control deep emotional feelings because they could affect their physical well-being.

One Three (3)

This number possesses great creative imagination and the ability to conceive far-reaching yet practical ideas. These people are equipped to cope with challenges and the problems of day-to-day life, as they have the natural ability to take the optimistic rather than the pessimistic approach. They are morally strong and will always protect and aid close friends throughout life.

One Nine (9)

No specific interpretation.

FULL AND MISSING LINES

One, Two, and Three (1–2–3) Full Thought Line

This denotes persons who seek to live in an orderly, organized fashion. Because tidiness is of prime importance to these people, they require others around them to maintain this level, but ironically they frequently fail to fulfill this character trait themselves. Consequently, misunderstandings and conflicts can occur, as they fail to practice what they preach. Persons possessing this combination have the ability to plan vast business enterprises and effect efficient control. They must learn to consider and evaluate even the smallest tasks as being important and essential to their final goal. This tendency frequently undermines their business expertise, but this can be overcome if they learn to delegate duties and responsibilities to those around them.

Basically, they are thoughtful people, but during times of pressure and crisis they tend to overlook totally the needs of others. This unfortunate trait arises because they are totally absorbed in their own enterprises and schemes, thus leaving little time to consider the plight of others. However, when sadness and grief are brought to their attention, this same mind power is then redirected to seek an effective solution. Needless to say, a person possessing this combination could be a good friend in times of need, provided, first, that the problem is of some magnitude, and, second, that he or she is made absolutely clear that it does exist.

Four, Five, and Six (4–5–6) Missing Will Line

This is an unfortunate configuration, as it often indicates family or home separations. It can also point to a somewhat strained relationship or alienation from one or both parents during childhood. This frequently occurs through parents being overly protective or too dominant in their attitude, thus suppressing the child's independence and natural enthusiasm. People possessing this missing line would generally suffer from lack of willpower and the inclination to give up a task at the first sign of opposition. Bearing this factor in mind, it comes as no surprise to find problems occurring in home and marriage, as these people lack the necessary tenacity and dedication so essential to a successful marriage or partnership. If they are able to realize this weakness and rectify it during early years, the chance of these problems occurring is greatly diminished.

They usually require somebody behind them in both home and business affairs, and it is of prime importance that people without these numbers in their chart associate with go-ahead, decision-making types who can complement the above weaknesses.

MISSING SINGLE NUMBERS

Seven (7) Missing

This signifies lack of spiritual expression and nonacceptance of metaphysical facts. It also shows a somewhat disorganized approach to life, seeking to stumble from day to day rather than planning for the future. A missing Seven also indicates a tendency in those missing this number to be inconsiderate of other people's opinions and feelings; they choose to ignore advice and prefer to make their own decisions regardless of conflicting circumstances. They must pay attention to health, diet, and nonabuse of the body, as their natural physical resistance is not strong.

Eight (8) Missing

This shows lack of business efficiency and financial ability. It is common to find individuals with an Eight missing from their natal chart to be both careless with money and illogical in their judgment of same. It is essential that these people appoint an accountant or qualified individual to handle their financial affairs, especially if they are self-employed or in a position of authority.

Those who are missing Eights seldom finish tasks and continually leave loose ends untied. High points in life must be consolidated on; otherwise material rewards could well be lost very quickly. Reliance on other people is common, due to their lack of self-confidence and fear of tackling tasks independently. These people need constant motivation, as the tendency to become lazy is very apparent.

LIFE PATH NUMBER INTERPRETATION

A Positive One Person
INDEPENDENT, ACTIVE, ORIGINAL, AMBITIOUS, COURAGEOUS

Positive Ones abound in creative inspiration and possess the ability to take others far beyond their normal, workable limits. This drive and action come directly from their enormous, inbuilt physical strength. As one would expect, determination is one of their most common traits, making them a force to contend with in both private and business life.

They are life's natural leaders with a flair for taking charge of any situation. They possess great originality, so it comes as no surprise to find many inventors and innovators born under this number. The gift of coupling a unique approach to standard practice provides the golden key to success with this highly ambitious number.

A Negative One Person
STUBBORN, LAZY, SELFISH, DICTATORIAL

Because this basic number is one of power, the negative traits are equally as powerful. As a result, these people are inclined to be very stubborn and lazy in both home and business and selfish to the point of being totally inconsiderate of others. Once a negative person of this number has made a decision, nothing would ever change his or her viewpoint, let alone the admission of defeat or failure. Unfortunately, this character trait drives many negative number Ones to follow the wrong path through to the bitter end, bringing about the downfall of themselves and others associated with them.

An Average One Person

These people possess all of the above positive and negative traits to a more passive degree, but even average individuals born with this number have the natural gift of leadership, coupled with the desire to be independent at all times. This trait leads to a very high percentage preferring to rule rather than be ruled. Although they make excellent employers, in most cases they make intolerable employees.

Home, Marriage, and Partners

Both male and female of this number prefer to adopt unconventional attitudes toward love, marriage, and home. Life can be exciting living with those of this number, as they are definitely not creatures of habit. They abhor system and normal routine; consequently, decisions concerning the home front are usually made very quickly and seemingly without a great deal of prior thought.

Because of their definite set of likes and dislikes and their desire to be in charge, marriage and partnerships can be turbulent. These people usually combine very adequately with personalities less dominant than themselves, thus allowing them to take command of most situations. Choice of partners for this number must be made with a great deal of thought and should be pretested for compatibility. As expected, the combination of two such dominant people together could produce disastrous results.

Suitable Occupations

It is natural for persons with this number to strive to be self-employed. By doing so, they are able to take advantage of their natural desire to make their own decisions and to rise or fall accordingly. It is essential that, if working for somebody else, an occupation be sought whereby a reasonable amount of autonomy and freedom of decision-making can be given. If given rein they can produce outstanding results, which, coupled with their physical strength, allows them to work under considerable stress for long periods.

Innovators, inventors, promoters, executives, organizers are all suitable occupations for this number. They also excel in positions of responsibility within the armed forces, as here their leadership ability can be utilized to the full. Their originality in any field of endeavor will ultimately lead to success.

DAY NUMBER CHARACTERISTICS

Twelfth Day (12)

This number shows a great love of life, coupled with the desire for action. Possessing great magnetism and imagination, persons with this number have the ability to change other people's opinions to suit their own line of thought.

Their mission in life is usually fully known and realized, and their gift of imagination steers them adequately on the right course to success. Their life seems to follow a series of highs and lows, mostly caused through their desire for immediate action.

They are inclined to be distracted by tempting affairs (not necessarily romantic). They should not succumb to them, as their line of direction and ambition could be sadly affected.

From the total individual interpretation, we must now pick the key words from each individual aspect and place them within the following preparation chart.

Note: For the time being, forget the large triangular configuration with the three circles at each corner, as the significance of this is dealt with in the next chapter. Use only the small triangles in the top corner for the natal chart dissection.

Key Word Preparation Chart

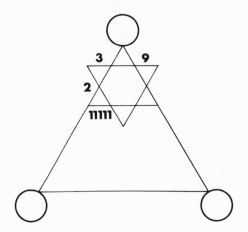

Name _____

Date of Birth: Month 11   Day 12   Year 1931

Life Path Number = 19 = 10 = 1

ASPECTS SHOWN WITHIN THE NATAL CHART

(1) Number of digits   5   Overtaxing physical energy, difficulty in relaxing, strong speech expression, overpowering attitude, strong basic desires, over-indulgence, literary and artistic fields suitable outlet for pent-up energy, dramatic results achieved in short space of time

(2) Number of digits   1   Can detect insincerity, immediate opinions formed, sensitive and intuitive, prone to emotional hardships, emotional feelings must be controlled

(3) Number of digits   1   Creative imagination, optimistic attitude, morally strong

(4) Number of digits   0   No aspect shown

(5) Number of digits   0   No aspect shown

(6) Number of digits   0   No aspect shown

(7) Number of digits   0   No aspect shown

(8) Number of digits   0   No aspect shown

(9) Number of digits   1   No specific interpretation

135

FULL AND MISSING LINES WITHIN THE NATAL CHART

Thought line (1–2–3) full   Desire order around them, can conceive and plan schemes, must pay attention to detail, must learn to delegate responsibilities, tend to overlook the needs of others

Will line (4–5–6) missing   Family and home problems experienced, strained relationships during childhood, lack of willpower, concedes too easily, needs motivation, must associate with go-ahead people

Action line (7–8–9) full or missing   No aspect shown

Mind line (3–6–9) full or missing   No aspect shown

Soul line (2–5–8) full or missing   No aspect shown

Physical line (1–4–7) full or missing   No aspect shown

Determination line (1–5–9) full or missing   No aspect shown

Compassion line (3–5–7) full or missing   No aspect shown

MISSING SINGLE NUMBERS WITHIN THE NATAL CHART

(1)   No specific interpretation

(2)   No aspect shown

(3)   No aspect shown

(4)   Shown in missing will line interpretation

(5)   Shown in missing will line interpretation

(6)   Shown in missing will line interpretation

(7)   Inability to cope with situations, lack of action, laziness, must pay attention to health, inability to analyze situations

(8)   Lack of action, ambition, and money ability, must finish tasks

(9)   No aspect shown

LIFE PATH NUMBER CHARACTERISTICS

Positive   Independent, active, original, ambitious, courageous, determined, great physical strength, life's natural leaders, unique approach to life

Negative   Stubborn, lazy, selfish, dictatorial, inconsiderate of others

Average   Independence required at all times, leadership sought, excellent employers, intolerable employees

Home, marriage, and partners   Unconventional attitudes, not creatures of habit, quick decisions made, marriages can be turbulent, definite likes and dislikes, associations with less dominant people suggested, partners must be chosen wisely

Suitable occupations   Should be self-employed, freedom and autonomy sought, must be allowed to make own decisions, originality, can work under stress, positions of responsibility preferred

DAY NUMBER CHARACTERISTICS

Twelfth day   Action, love of life, imagination, can change others' opinions, frequent highs and lows experienced, could be attracted to tempting affairs

---

The preparation chart is for our own use to enable us to group all the key words under their respective headings. It is now a simple process to evaluate the information shown, picking out the common denominators which will enable us eventually to compile a short, concise, understandable resume for the individual in question.

The following list illustrates the common denominators and resume pointers that evolve from the preparation chart.

Common Denominator Synopsis

1. This person frequently overlooks the needs of others.
2. Lack of action and willpower are evident, together with a constant need for motivation.

3. Tasks must be pursued from conception through to completion, as the tendency to give up too easily is very apparent.
4. Family and home problems are evident, as this person lacks the tenacity to make associations successful. Friends and business associates must be chosen wisely, with emphasis placed on bright, go-ahead company.
5. Freedom of decision-making and positions of responsibility are essential.
6. Because of their unique approach and unconventional attitude toward life, they tend to abhor mundane, day-to-day routine.
7. Although positions of responsibility and self-employment should be sought, it is essential that other people be utilized to provide strength within the areas of finance, motivation, organization, and implementation.
8. The ability to make quick decisions is apparent.
9. Definite sets of likes and dislikes are shown.
10. Overtaxing of physical and mental energy is clearly indicated. Suggested outlets for this pent-up energy are the literary or artistic fields.
11. The ability to achieve dramatic results within a short space of time is apparent.
12. The ability to work under pressure is evident.
13. Personal strength lies within the areas of creative imagination and organization.
14. The gift of conceiving and planning schemes shows clearly. However, the necessary tenacity to follow these schemes through is not apparent.
15. The tendency to be overbearing and dictatorial must be avoided, as dependency on others to effect success is apparent.
16. The ability to detect insincerity in others is clearly shown.
17. Due to a forceful, dominant personality that unfortunately lacks drive and tenacity, frequent highs and lows can be experienced throughout life.

From the seventeen given common denominators and resume pointers, we can now compile our final chart analysis, which should be divided into five separate sections:

1. General personal resume
2. Negative points to be overcome
3. Vocational guidance pointers

4. Pyramid years
5. Vibrations for this year
6. Vibrations for next year

Note: The last two sections are dealt with in the next chapter.

Let us now look at the final natal chart resume to see how it would be presented to the individual in question.

Final Natal Chart Resume

Name _____

Date of Birth: Month: 11; Day: 12; Year: 1931
        Life Path Number = 19 = 10 = 1

General Personal Resume
The general attributes associated with the life path number One are enjoyed within your chart, as the desire to rule rather than to be ruled is very apparent. However, due to several inherent negative character traits, caution must be exercised in daily life; otherwise opportunities that are rightfully yours will not be forthcoming.

Your forte lies within the area of creative imagination, as you have the natural ability to conceive far-reaching plans and schemes. But it is of the utmost importance that you surround yourself with qualified people who can substitute their strength in your areas of weaknesses (see negative points to be overcome). The ability to achieve dramatic results within a very short space of time is apparent, but you must learn to stabilize and capitalize on your efforts; otherwise life will be a series of ups and downs. You abound in mental and physical energy, but you must be careful not to overtax yourself. A suitable outlet for this pent-up energy must be found, and in your case the literary or artistic fields offer the most suitable vehicles.

You must try to avoid becoming dictatorial and overbearing in your speech and attitude toward others, as your dependence on friends and associates is very important to your effective, day-to-day existence and future. Your unconventional attitude toward love, marriage, and home is a general trait of all number Ones, but you must realize that society does invoke some restrictions and boundaries. These limitations are imposed not to suppress individuality but to create livable harmony.

You possess the natural ability to detect insincerity in others, and as such, you make friends very quickly; luckily, your judgment is rarely proven wrong. Problems associated with home, marriage, and during childhood are evident. These can be overcome when you realize that marriages and partnerships have to be worked on and that the desire to give should hold greater significance than the desire to take. You must surround yourself with go-ahead people, as you require constant motivation and stimulation.

Negative Points to Be Overcome

Your natal chart shows great strength in certain areas, but also shows many negative points that you should endeavor to overcome. You should at all times try to consider the needs of others around you, realizing that you alone cannot achieve your aims and ambitions. "What you sow, so shall you reap" is a saying worth remembering, as help and consideration given to others will be repaid tenfold throughout your life.

Your goals must be set very clearly and should be pursued with tenacity and dedication, as lack of action, willpower, and drive show very clearly within your chart. Your love of freedom must be somewhat stabilized, as it is impossible to go through life without having responsibilities placed on your shoulders.

You must learn to respect the opinions and desires of others close to you, realizing that, like you, they also require a degree of freedom, action, and expression.

Vocational Guidance Pointers

Your vocation or employment must be chosen very carefully, as the desire for autonomy and freedom of decision-making shows very clearly. Great success from self-employment could be enjoyed, *provided* you realize your weaknesses and employ or associate with others who can impart their strength and wisdom in these areas. You must avoid becoming a jack-of-all-trades and master of none, realizing that delegation of responsibility is an important factor in the business world.

The ability to handle money is not apparent within your chart. Therefore, you must give attention to financial matters and planning. You give of your best when working under conditions of pressure; consequently, any occupation involving constant deadlines or time limitation would be suitable.

Partnerships or family businesses are not advisable in your case, as working with those close to you could not only create an unharmonious business environment, but could also endanger future relationships. Your ability to conceive original and imaginative ideas can be valuable in many areas. Look for suitable challenges and then allow this natural talent to take effect. It is an unusual gift to possess and one that you should dedicate yourself toward using to the full.

Pyramid Years
Your natal chart indicates that the following ages in your life will prove to be significant: 26, 35, 44, 53.

Vibrations for This Year
See next chapter.

Vibrations for Next Year
See next chapter.

Remember, as you begin to do personal analysis, perseverance and dedication are required more than ever. The task at hand may seem insurmountable, but practice does make perfect and rest assured that as time progresses the process will become second nature and the whole natal analysis will unfold within a matter of minutes. Practice this chart analysis on yourself, friends, relatives, and loved ones. Read and reread these chapters until you know each aspect interpretation by heart, because in doing so your task will become easier as your knowledge and understanding of the subject increase.

The headings dealing with the vibrations for this year and next year were left blank because the following chapter deals with the method required to evaluate the total vibrations. The current and forthcoming vibrations *cannot* be calculated or interpreted correctly until the natal analysis is known. Thus, the reason for this chapter appearing after the total complete chart analysis.

10

The Harmonics of Life

The Power of Rhythm

Much can be achieved by those who are in harmony with their very being; likewise frustrations and restrictions can be experienced by creating discords within the natural rhythm of the universe.

Rhythm is the pulse of life that affects every living organism on this earth. Man is now beginning to realize the enormous importance of natural rhythm by utilizing and harnessing it for the good of mankind. Yet in an indirect fashion, man has taken advantage of the power of rhythm and harmony for many thousands of years.

Rhythmic chanting has been used throughout history to create an awareness or atmosphere. We have long seen natives moving to a fixed rhythmical beat, inducing a hypnotic state whereby extraordinary physical feats can be accomplished. The beat of war drums rising to a crescendo transforms placid individuals into crazed, potential killers. Soldiers marching long distances are encouraged to sing powerful, rhythmical songs to enable their bodies to establish a pattern of habit, to reduce physical exhaustion, and to create united moral support. Distance athletes plan their races in advance, by using the rhythm of numbers to provide a pattern of pace, again establishing a mental/physical habit designed to push their body beyond the normal limits of endurance. Crowds at sports events chant in unison to encourage their local team, again creating a singular rhythm of purpose.

Nature does not confine the wonders of rhythm to man alone. Plants also respond to these influences; experiments have shown that their growth rate increases dramatically when they are placed within a musically harmonious environment. Harmony, through the vehicle of music,

142

has uplifted man to wonderful, far-reaching heights, but has also reduced him to the lowest depths of despair—such is the power of rhythm.

Rhythm has *always* been significant in Numerology, as it utilizes personal and universal vibrations to establish a pattern of circumstance. If people are in harmony with their very being, then the chances of success must be increased threefold.

Use of the Harmony Triangle

By combining the life path number with the personal and universal year numbers, we are able to see at a glance whether a person is in harmony with his or her personal and universal vibrations for any given year.

As we now know, an individual's life path number signifies his or her destiny in life, a destiny that can remain throughout a life span, or can change according to situations and circumstances. The universal year number provides a vibration that affects each living person, whereas the personal year number holds significance singularly for a specific individual during any one year of his or her life. The life path number obviously remains the same throughout life, but personal and universal year sequences change each year.

To record these three major vibrations, we use a triangle as an easy means to highlight these factors.

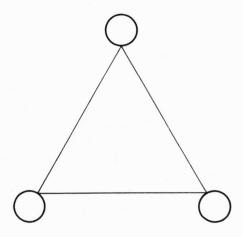

Let's look at an individual born on 12/18/28 to see how his or her vibrations influence them during the year 1977:

    a. Life path number = 5

    b. Universal year number = 6

    c. Personal year number = 9

We can now place these numbers in the triangle shown below:

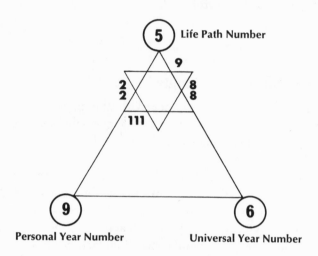

You will notice that the top corner of the triangle includes the natal chart dissection. This is because greater emphasis should be placed on the strong and weak points of the individual rather than on the life path number. From knowledge gained in the previous chapter, we should be able to provide the necessary resumes covering the life path number, natal analysis, and personal and universal year numbers. These resumes can now be listed as shown below.

Natal Chart Resume (Condensed Analysis)

This indicates emotional, intuitive, and highly sensitive persons who must be prepared to give of themselves in matters of home and marriage. A tendency toward laziness exists, as does the need for constant motivation. Responsibilities should be borne and not avoided. Frequent complications could occur as a result of a bombastic, dictatorial attitude that must be tempered. This person should seek to place more emphasis on spiritual rewards than on material gains. Lack of willpower is clearly indicated, together with a tendency to be restless by nature. Their choice of friends is often questionable. Consequently, it is essential that they associate with bright, happy people. Writing talent is evident, but some difficulty with speech expression could be experienced.

A Six (6) Universal Year

Harmony of world conditions will be the theme during this period, together with thoughts of the home, children, and the underprivileged.

A Nine (9) Personal Year

This is a stocktaking year when values and ideals must be carefully scrutinized. Giving to others should hold far greater significance than keeping for oneself during this period. Relationships and associations are important now, as is the awareness of nonmaterial "free" benefits of life. This is a consolidation year when existing schemes and plans must be completed, ready for a new nine-year cycle. A total giving year.

We must now closely inspect and dissect the above resumes to ascertain whether (a) the person, (b) the universal year, and (c) the personal year vibrations are in harmony. The following brief conclusions can now be reached:

The Person

Materially conscious, needs motivation. Lacks spiritual awareness, drive, ambition, and willpower. Home and family complications . . .

in a

Universal Year

When harmonious conditions, together with the unity of people, children, and family, are paramount . . .

in a

Personal Year

Where giving becomes a fact of life, together with an awakening to and realization of spiritual matters.

The above clearly shows that the vibrations of this individual during the year 1977 are somewhat out of character with the life path and natal resume. Therefore we can readily come to the following final conclusion:

Influencing vibrations for a person born on 12/18/1928 during the year 1977:

This will be a year in which material gains will be secondary to home affairs. An awakening to spiritual matters will occur, with the result that previously accepted ideals and paths will be questioned. Although there have been problems associated with home, marriage, and children, there will now be a greater understanding and a desire to unite rather than separate.

Increased physical and mental effort is required during this year, as the general vibrations are not ones of ambition. This factor, coupled with an inherent lack of willpower, could create financial and business problems. Frustrations and lack of identity could occur, as the unharmonious interaction of seeking to give as well as requiring to take creates mental turmoil.

The variations and combinations that could occur among these three factors are enormous, plus the fact that more emphasis should be placed on the individual natal interpretations than the life path number. Consequently, it would be impractical to list each possible combination. However, the following combinations and table provide a useful guide when calculating vibrations for any given year.

COMBINATION 1

Any year in which all three factors, i.e., life path number, universal and personal year numbers, are identical should produce complete harmony of purpose and individuality of expression.

Example

An individual born on 4/5/1945 during the year 1972:

    a. Life path number = 1
    b. Universal year for 1972 = 1
    c. Personal year for 1972 = 1

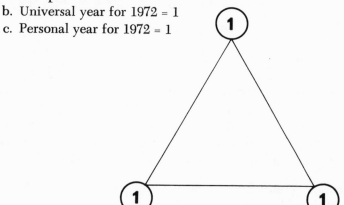

Note: When this combination occurs with any given number, the general theme of that number shares a common ground with all three factors. Although we expressed the viewpoint above that it indicates a harmonious year, the total analysis would depend largely on the number or person in question.

COMBINATION 2

Any year in which the life path number and personal year number are identical should produce unity of purpose that would depend on the restrictions or enhancement of the universal year vibration.

Example

    An individual born on 6/7/1944 during the year 1971:

        a. Life path number = 4
        b. Universal year for 1971 = 9
        c. Personal year for 1971 = 4

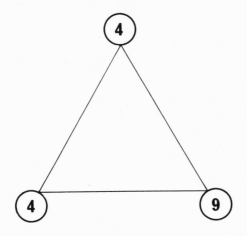

COMBINATION 3

Any year in which the life path and universal year numbers are identical should produce unity of thought and desire, but again depending on the personal year vibration as to whether these thoughts will be transformed into action.

Example

    An individual born on 7/24/1940 during the year 1980:

a. Life path number = 9
b. Universal year for 1980 = 9
c. Personal year for 1980 = 4

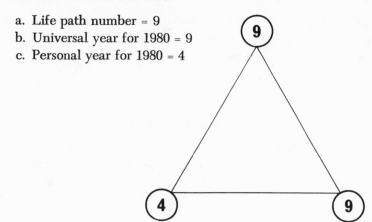

COMBINATION 4

Any year in which the personal and universal year numbers are identical should produce unity of action and purpose that could, or could not, be out of character with the life path number and natal analysis.

Example

An individual born on 9/18/1942 during the year 1974:

a. Life path number = 7
b. Universal year for 1974 = 3
c. Personal year for 1974 = 3

COMBINATION 5

Any year in which all three factors are different should produce vibrations that could be harmonious or unharmonious, depending largely on the numbers in question.

Example

For an individual born on 5/10/1958 during the year 1969:

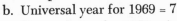

    a. Life path number = 1
    b. Universal year for 1969 = 7
    c. Personal year for 1969 = 4

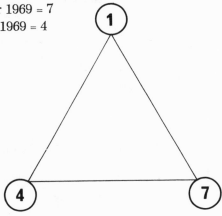

Note: (a) It is worth noting that if an individual possesses a birth date that offers an identical life path, universal and personal year number (as shown in the first example), the personal and universal numbers will fall into uniform progression. The identical combination of these factors will create a cycle which commences at the year of birth and repeats every nine years. The old saying that some people are born lucky although not exactly true as it applies to material gains alone is verified somewhat by the above fact. (b) It is important to remember that the natal analysis holds greater significance than does the life path number. Some persons could possess character traits out of keeping with their life path number. Then again, some people do fit snugly into the general interpretations. The accuracy of this method depends largely on your ability to define the person in question, as the significance and consequences of the vibrations produced depend totally on an individual analysis. This point alone was responsible for this chapter being placed after the total chart analysis.

Harmony Table

The Harmony Table lists the three factors of life path, universal, and personal year vibrations. They should be used as an aid in interpreting the various sequences that can occur.

Life Path—Universal—Personal Combination Table

(To be used as a guide only)

Life Path Number		Universal Year Number	Personal Year Number
(1)	Original	Optimism, looking to the future	Strength and independence
(2)	Analytical	Consolidation and cooperation	Patience and togetherness
(3)	Artistic	Inspirational expression	Happy outward awareness
(4)	Durable	Effective organization	Effort and hard work
(5)	Freedom	Collective associations	Exuberant restlessness
(6)°	Benevolent	Harmonious stability	Romantic awareness
(7)	Service	Consolidation and perfection	Waiting and restrictions
(8)	Powerful	Prosperity and expansion	Realization of rewards
(9)	Generous	Humanistic unselfishness	Innermost stocktaking
(11)†	Inspirational	Spiritual awareness	Pursuit of spiritual matters
(22)†	Supremacy	Universal expansion and obligations	Inspirational activity
(33)	Tolerant		Physical awareness

° Six is a harmonious, stabilizing number; therefore it creates excellent vibrations with all other combinations.

† Master numbers 11 and 22 add strength and harmony of purpose to any other combination.

Let's now look at some examples to see how the table provides a speedy and effective method of establishing various individual vibrations. Bear in mind that the natal chart resume has not been included in these examples; therefore the accuracy at this stage is questionable.

Example 1

To find the harmonious vibrations for an individual born on 3/14/43 during the year 1981:

a. Life path number = 7
b. Universal year number = 1
c. Personal year number = 9

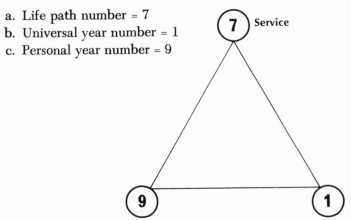

Innermost Stocktaking   Optimism, Looking to the Future

Conclusion: These persons seek to be of service to the community and as such would find that their schemes and ideas relating to others would be accepted with a degree of optimism by the general public. They would desire to question present ideals, looking from within for the answers. This is a good year, when harmony of purpose and ambition reign supreme, coupled with the desire to consider the future and forget the past.

Example 2

To find the harmonious vibrations for an individual born on 6/28/1951 during the year 1974:

a. Life path number = 5
b. Universal year number = 3
c. Personal year number = 1

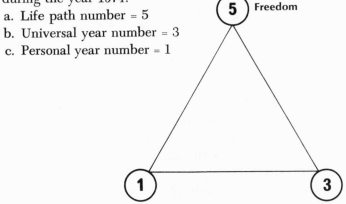

Strength and Independence   Inspirational Expression

Conclusion: This should prove to be an exceptional year wherein the desire to express individuality is strengthened by a feeling of physical adequacy and originality. The confidence and ability to push ahead provides an excellent basis for commencement of any new venture. Success is assured, provided the scheme or idea in question involves people. A get-up-and-go year.

Example 3

To find the harmonious vibrations for an individual born on 6/11/1922 during the year 1979:

a. Life path number = 22
b. Universal year number = 8
c. Personal year number = 7

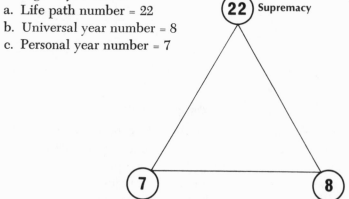

Waiting and Restriction   Prosperity and Expansion

Conclusion: The ability to initiate far-reaching aims and ambitions should be highlighted during this year. The general vibrations of prosperity and expansion provide a suitable, acceptable vehicle for new schemes and ventures. However, the personal year is one of waiting and consolidation rather than drive and action. Consequently, frustrations could occur this year as the desire to push ahead is wagered against an apparent lack of opportunity. Emphasis must not be placed on personal material gains, as rewards of a spiritual nature are more likely to occur.

Note: As we expressed previously, the above examples and conclusions have been derived from the life path number and do not include the natal chart resume. They have been included to illustrate the general method and do not represent accurate assessments. It would be an excellent exercise to construct the natal chart of each of these examples to see how the resume would affect the general conclusion.

However concise or explicit a Numerologist may be in his or her evaluation of a subject, numerous questions obviously arise as a result of information given. So to alleviate this problem, we have included a series of probable questions, together with their respective answers. So turn now to the next chapter to see the type of questions that you, the future Numerologist, will invariably be asked.

11

For Each Question There Is an Answer

When engaged in conversation with a person knowledgeable in any given field, it is gratifying to raise a question and be given a sensible, accurate, down-to-earth answer immediately. Confidence and admiration are strengthened as we come to the conclusion that he or she really does know the subject.

Throughout history men and women have studied Numerology and other occult arts. They served a long, hard, grueling apprenticeship, and their services were never rendered to others until their knowledge had been proven. Unfortunately, this has changed dramatically during the last century. For although awareness of occult subjects is increasing each day, unqualified tutoring and piecemeal information have resulted in thousands of ill-informed, do-it-yourself Numerologists, Astrologers, and Clairvoyants. Knowledge of the twelve signs of the Astrological zodiac, together with their respective meanings, does not produce a qualified Astrologer. Likewise, knowledge of the twelve signs of the Numerological zodiac and their respective interpretations does not produce a Numerologist. But sadly, the world is full of people who advise others on these ancient subjects with little or no knowledge themselves.

It is not surprising that, if these people reach a certain level of notoriety, they instinctively cultivate the knack of evading certain questions. The reason for this evasion is simple—the answer is not known. To be asked a straightforward question and evade the answer simply shows a lack of knowledge. Yet one can see this occurring each day of each week of each year. It comes as no surprise that many people form the opinions that these subjects are *not* based on good, solid logic and reasoning.

We sincerely hope that you do not join the ever-increasing numbers of ill-informed occult experts, but that you use this book as a jump-ing-off point for your spiritual studies as you endeavor to find knowledge and enlightenment.

The minute you practice this ancient art you are classed as a Nu-merologist; not a trainee or an apprentice Numerologist, but simply a Numerologist. As such, then, it is important that you know the answers to at least some of the questions that will undoubtedly be fired at you.

If you do not know the answer to a question, don't try to evade or sidestep the issue. Simply say that your stage of learning has not reached a significant enough level to be able to answer the question accurately. It is better to admit this fact than to make up an illogical, on-the-spot answer, or evade the issue completely.

Generally, people will respect your sincerity and honesty in ad-mitting that you do not know the answer. They will also realize that Nu-merology is a very intricate and profound subject that requires years of dedicated learning to enable one to be termed an expert.

So to arm you in your future endeavors, we have devoted a chapter to the common, not-so-common, and rare questions that you are likely to be asked, together with their respective answers.

Question: I have twins born on the same day; does this mean that their Numerological charts will be identical?

Answer: Their natal chart analysis would be identical, but this covers only one side of a full Numerological reading. Calculations derived from the full given name create destiny, soul urge, and quiescent self-vibrations. Therefore their charts would differ on total analysis.

(Note: See Chapter 10 for reference to above vibrations.)

Question: I was born three weeks premature. How does Numerology cope with this factor?

Answer: You were born on the day nature intended and as such your premature arrival does not hold any significance in Numerology. Your life path number is calculated on your actual date of birth, not from the estimated arrival date. This date is man-made.

Question: Can Numerology tell me about my future?

Answer: Your future largely depends on what you do today. If you pre-pare and equip yourself for future happenings then you will be ready to take advantage of them when they occur. If you lead a negative life in the present then you must expect negative results in the future. Similarly, if you lead a positive life than you can expect and will rightfully receive future positive results.

Numerology allows one to calculate and interpret the vibrations and number patterns that are likely to occur throughout life. Man is truly master of his own destiny, but by utilizing your natural talents, being aware of your negative influences, and combining the Numerological yearly, monthly, and daily vibrations, you can reach a prescribed peak or destiny. But attitudes, circumstances, influences, and outside stimuli frequently change our path in life, automatically creating a new personal destiny.

The following explanation may serve to illustrate clearly the use of Numerology:

If you imagine the body to be a tuning fork (as used in music to establish a note), the fork has been tapped and is held in the hand where it vibrates, yet it does not emit a sound—this is a body constantly vibrating in personal rhythm with its very being.

When the fork is placed face down on a table, the sound of its vibration will be emitted for all to hear. When the body reacts within a harmonious environment or pattern, it, like the tuning fork, emits vibrations and bursts forth for all to see and hear. The vibrations take effect and then wane as the rhythm reduces in power—like the tuning fork as it ceases to vibrate.

If one is aware of the universal and personal vibrations that are likely to occur within any given day, month, or year, then this knowledge can be put to good personal use.

If man's individual future were planned to the finest detail, there would be no obstacles to overcome, no challenges to meet, and above all no purpose in life. Each one of us was born an individual, and it is our purpose in life to realize this individuality and serve ourselves and humanity accordingly. Numerology does provide the golden key to individual and universal rhythms, but it does not provide the hand to turn that key—you alone do.

Question: Why am I totally opposite to the definition of my life path number?

Answer: Your life path number is a generalization and holds far less significance than your natal chart analysis. Consequently you may be a number Six by birth, but possess qualities more closely allied to a number One.

Question: Can Numerology tell me how long I will live?

Answer: How long do you want to live? Numerology says that the quality of life holds greater significance than the quantity of years. By utilizing all of your senses, satisfaction from life will be gained, but this can never be measured in numbers of years.

Question: Can Numerology tell me how many children I will have?

Answer: Numerology endorses the old saying that it is not the man in your life, but the life in your man that will determine this. (Refer to the question and answer that relates to the future.)

Question: When do the personal years commence?

Answer: The personal year vibrations usually commence from January each year and last for a period of twelve months. However, there is one notable exception, that of a Three life path number during a Three personal year. This vibration lasts for a period of eighteen months, thus reducing the following Four personal year to a period of only six months. Our experience and research have proven that, when an individual enters a personal year number identical to their life path number, the influences of this harmonious action tend to increase the duration of the personal year vibration.

Question: Do Numerology and Astrology reach the same conclusions about an individual?

Answer: Through two vastly different sets of calculations and interpretations, a singular result can often occur. Many common denominators can be found within the two subjects; indeed most Astrologers utilize Numerology in some form to aid their analysis.

Question: Does the time of my birth affect my life path number?

Answer: No. Numerology does not require the time or place of birth, only the date of birth.

Question: Why, when I was told by one Numerologist that my birth number was Six, do you now tell me that my life path number is Four? My date of birth is 3/24/1948.

Answer: There are many different schools of Numerology, one of which calculates the life path number upon the day of birth only. Consequently, according to that system your life path number would be Six. But our experience and constant experimentation have proven that the life path number must relate to the full date of birth.

Question: You tell me that I should enjoy excellent health because I have the numbers One, Four, and Seven in my chart. But I have been sick for the past two years.

Answer: Your natal chart represents you as an individual, unprogrammed, uncluttered and unaffected by society. The numbers One, Four, and Seven show that you possess an inbuilt strength and should enjoy reasonable health throughout life. Most problems are self-induced and health is no exception. Abuse of the body, lack of exercise, incorrect diet, anxieties, inhibitions, and pent-up emotions can all affect our physical health and well-being. The inherent stamina is there within your chart, but could have been overpowered by the above influences.

Question: I have been told that if I change my name I will alter the vibrations that affect my life.

Answer: By changing your name you can certainly alter the vibrations that affect your personality, but it depends largely on what you seek from life. It is a very lengthy task to evaluate the total significance of a name change, as letters, vowels, and consonants are all considered and add to the total interpretation and significance. Throughout history people have changed or shortened their name to create a specific vibration or influence.

Question: I have been told that I should look for someone with a number Five in his or her chart. Why?

Answer: Your natal chart shows that you are missing the number Five from your date of birth. Five is a very important number in Numerology, as it represents the center pivot of the whole natal chart and as such is rightly called the mixing or motivating number. By combining your talents with a person who does possess a number Five in his or her birth date, your strong points will be increased and your weak points diminished. You need a push in life and these people can provide just that.

Question: How does Numerology establish compatibility between two people?

Answer: Each number from One to Nine holds an individual significance, and from these numbers and groups of numbers, we are able to establish your character analysis, highlighting strong points, weak points, likes, and dislikes.

Compatibility in Numerology is a simple factor to establish. The law of science that says like poles repel, unlike poles attract is also followed in Numerology. Consequently if one person possesses strength in his or her chart where another has weakness, or vice versa, then these two people should prove to be harmonious and compatible. But compatibility comparisons require a great deal of analysis, as many factors must be taken into consideration.

12
Fact Not Fiction

Throughout this book we have referred to Numerology as being a now subject. We are more concerned with the present and the future than we are with the past. History imparts knowledge so that man can learn how to live with himself and his fellowmen. This is obviously an idealistic approach, as history has repeatedly shown that man has never learned how to live in harmony with his fellowmen. Still, it is hoped that one day he will see the light and use history in its true perspective—that of providing a wealth of practical and worthy experience. As children, we touch fire and burn our fingers; thus we learn that fire is both dangerous and painful, and that we must expect the same consequences if we touch fire in the future. The past track record of man has been far from impressive, for he continually touches fire. He cannot be excused for his lack of experience, as history has taught the consequences that can be expected.

It is not the desire of the authors to evaluate man's spiritual evolution. However, this book would not be complete without at least looking at some past events to see if they were Numerologically significant. The astute reader realizes that if we spent endless weeks researching significant historical dates, sooner or later some would appear that held a Numerological connotation. He would also be aware that the authors, in their enthusiasm, would only illustrate dates that were correct in their Numerological significance. With full realization of this fact, we have chosen to discuss briefly one factor pertaining to the last two major world wars, including major events that happened throughout their duration.

We now know that the numbers One and Nine are commencing and finalizing numbers, both in personal and universal year, month, and day vibrations. Where one finishes, so another starts; therefore the opposite pattern can take effect. If a war were declared in a Nine universal year, it obviously indicates a finishing of previous conditions and the commencement of new ones. Therefore, the One and Nine universal years, months, and days are extremely important, as they signify a complete change of affairs and conditions. Bearing this in mind, it is interesting to look at relevant dates during these two world wars to see how these numbers occurred with above-average regularity. Do not overlook the fact that we have included in our calculations *all* the relevant dates (even though we only list the major ones) that occurred within that very short space of history.

FIRST WORLD WAR

Britain declared war on Germany
    on a *Nine* universal day.
Japan declared war on Germany
    on a *One* universal day.
Germany defeated the Russians at Tannenberg
    on a *Nine* universal day.
Germany ordered a submarine blockade of Britain
    on a *Nine* universal day.
The Allies landed at Gallipoli
    on a *Nine* universal day.
The Germans sank the Cunard liner *Lusitania*
    on a *One* universal day.
The Allies began evacuating Gallipoli
    in a *One* universal month.
Germany announced that merchant ships would be sunk without warning
    in a *One* universal month.
Great Britain adopted conscription
    on a *One* universal day.
The United States severed relationships with Germany
    in a *Nine* universal year.
U.S. President Woodrow Wilson asked Congress to arm merchant ships
    on a *One* universal day in a *Nine* universal year.
The United States declared war on Germany
    in a *Nine* universal year.
The United States adopted selective conscription
    on a *One* universal day in a *Nine* universal year.
The first U.S. troops landed in France
    in a *Nine* universal year.

The United States declared war on Austria and Hungary
    on a *One* universal day in a *Nine* universal year.
The fall of the Prussian Empire commenced
when its Navy and Army revolted
    in a *Nine* universal year . . .
And ended
    on a *Nine* universal day in a *Nine* universal year.
The Bolsheviks overthrew Kerenski
    on a *One* universal day in a *Nine* universal year.
Russia made peace with Germany
    in a *One* universal year.
President Wilson presented his Fourteen Points for peace
    on a *One* universal day in a *One* universal year.
Bulgaria conceded
    in a *One* universal month in a *One* universal year.
Austria surrendered
    in a *One* universal year.
The Armistice was signed
    in a *One* universal year.
The German fleet surrendered to the British Navy
    in a *One* universal year.

From 108 important dates that occurred within the period of the First World War, 64 of them occurred on a One or Nine universal day, month, or year number (this total does not include dates that had a multiple of universal numbers).

It is worth mentioning that certain significant dates occurred on multiple years, months, and days: The British broke through the Hindenburg Line on a day in which all three factors of the date were in the number One universal vibration. Great Britain adopted conscription on a One universal day, and America also adopted conscription on a One universal day. Not only were they identical in their Numerological significance, but each occurred within a Twenty-two universal month and these two dates were eleven months apart!

The Armistice was signed on the 11th day of the 11th month 1918 and the cease-fire bugle was blown at the 11th hour. We know that Eleven is a master number and signifies spiritual uplifting. Not only is this important, but the document was signed on a Five universal day, which signifies joining of people, in a Three universal month, which indicates inspired happiness, vision, and dreams of fulfillment.

Let's now look at the Second World War to see if the same pattern occurred.

SECOND WORLD WAR

Russia invaded Finland
    on a *Nine* universal day.
South Africa declared war on Germany
    on a *One* universal day.
Germany invaded Norway and Denmark
    on a *Nine* universal day in a *Nine* universal month.
The retreat from Dunkirk commenced
    on a *Nine* universal day in a *One* universal month.
Germany invaded the Netherlands, Belgium, and Luxembourg
    in a *One* universal month.
Britain declared war on Japan
    in a *Nine* universal month.
The Free French declared war on Japan
    in a *Nine* universal month.
Japan attacked Pearl Harbor
    in a *Nine* universal month.
Japan declared war on Great Britain, Australia, New Zealand,
Canada, and South Africa
    in a *Nine* universal month.
Germany and Italy declared war on the United States
    in a *Nine* universal month.
General Douglas MacArthur was ordered to leave the Philippines
    on a *Nine* universal day.
American General Jonathan Wainwright surrendered to the
Japanese troops
    on a *Nine* universal day.
The Battle of the Coral Sea commenced
    on a *One* universal day.
The United States declared war on Bulgaria, Hungary, and Rumania
    on a *Nine* universal day.
The Battle of Midway finished
    on a *One* universal day.
The German Army surrendered to the Russian troops at Stalingrad
    in a *Nine* universal month.

The Allies invaded France
in a *Nine* universal year.
Paris was liberated
in a *Nine* universal year.
Russia declared an armistice with Finland
on a *One* universal day in a *Nine* universal month
in a *Nine* universal year.
General MacArthur returned to the Philippines
in a *One* universal month in a *One* universal year.
The Battle of Leyte Gulf commenced
in a *One* universal month in a *Nine* universal year . . .
And ended
on a *One* universal day in a *One* universal month
in a *Nine* universal year.
The German drive was stopped
on a *One* universal day in a *Nine* universal year.
Okinawa was invaded
in a *One* universal year.
German armies began surrendering
on a *One* universal day in a *One* universal year.
V-E Day was
in a *One* universal year.
The United States dropped the atomic bomb on Hiroshima
in a *Nine* universal month in a *One* universal year.
Russia declared war on Japan
in a *Nine* universal month in a *One* universal year.
The United States dropped the atomic bomb on Nagasaki
in a *Nine* universal month in a *One* universal year.
Japan surrendered
in a *Nine* universal month in a *One* universal year.
V-J Day was
in a *One* universal month in a *One* universal year.

From the ninety significant dates that occurred in the Second World War, sixty of them were on a One or Nine universal day, month, or year (this does not include dates that held a multiple of universal numbers).

It is worth noting that similar to World War I, many significant dates occurred on multiple universal days, months, and years: Russia declared war on Japan in a Nine universal month within a One universal year. The retreat from Dunkirk occurred on a Nine universal day within a One universal month. General MacArthur returned to the Philippines in a One universal month within a Nine universal year. The German army began surrendering on a One universal day within a One universal year. Japan surrendered in a Nine universal month within a One universal year.

The following important Numerological dates also stand out: Russia declared an armistice with Finland on a One universal day in a Nine universal month within a Nine universal year. The battle of Leyte Gulf, which was the biggest naval action ever fought, finished on a One universal day in a One universal month within a Nine universal year. Lastly, the United States dropped the atom bomb on Nagasaki on a Nine universal day in a Nine universal month within a One universal year. This action, together with Hiroshima, hastened the Japanese surrender.

In view of these somewhat startling conclusions, it may not come as a surprise to find that three major events concerning both world wars, that of the signing of the armistice in the First World War, and V-E Day and the Japanese surrender in the Second World War, all occurred on Five universal days. Furthermore, both world wars finished in a One universal year. The number Five signifies joining of people, whereas the number One indicates a new beginning.

Pythagoras was indeed correct when he based his teachings on the philosophies that the universe existed on numbers.

13
Where Do We Go from Here?

If you have carefully and diligently followed the steps given in this book, you should be able to compile an accurate natal Numerological chart.

Technically we can now class you as a Numerologist. However, your knowledge and understanding of this subject are just beginning. Your new title indicates only that the first part of your apprenticeship has now been served.

Most people desire to further their knowledge of a subject that holds some appeal or curiosity for them. Their newfound information will serve to whet their appetite for further facts and knowledge.

The natal chart is based on an individual's date of birth and does not consider the person's given, married, or used names. The life path number analysis indicates an individual's destiny, but by including their names, we are also able to ascertain the following accurately: Soul urge (their true desires in life), quiescent self (their innermost individuality), and total name expression (their outward desires and existence).

So for the serious students who desire to increase their knowledge in this ancient, thought-provoking science, the following pointers may prove helpful.

Do not attempt to study other methods of Numerology relating to name vibrations until you have fully mastered the art of compiling and interpreting a natal chart as shown within the pages of this book. There are many different schools of Numerology employing varied methods, with the result that if the very basis of the subject is not fully understood, confusion can occur.

When you have reached a sufficient level of expertise, then, and only then, is the time to tour bookshops and libraries looking for other material on this subject.

Practice does make perfect, but as we mentioned in earlier chapters, your task as a Numerologist must not be taken lightly. You will be confronted by people who have had and possibly still have problems and difficulties within their lives. To advise these people is a great responsibility and one that cannot be upheld with little care for mankind.

14

Who Is to Blame?

You are probably wondering why a book on the subject of Numerology should include chapters dealing with mental conditioning and motivation. At first glance it does perhaps seem an odd combination. However, if you examine the reason behind this inclusion, you will see that it is a very logical progression.

Each day of the year, we, as Numerologists, analyze the charts of many individuals. We meet and dissect successful, unsuccessful, worried, troubled, frustrated, happy, sad, contented, logical, and illogical people from all walks of life. Therefore, our assumptions are based on *actual* and *factual* experience. We do not consider ourselves to be psychiatrists or psychoanalysts. However, we do consider ourselves to be accurate, experienced judges of people and their complexities. Our studies over the years have drawn us to make the following conclusions:

That the majority of people are:

1. Unaware of their true purpose in life,
   or
2. Unhappy with their day-to-day existence,
   or
3. Totally unaware of their talents or potential,
   or
4. Completely negative and pessimistic in their approach to life,
   or
5. Living a humdrum unexciting existence,
   or
6. Questioning their very being.

This book is about people, their desires, ambitions, purpose, and feelings in life. We cannot turn a blind eye or overlook the above conclusions as they are so detrimental to our very way of life.

So with this reasoning in mind, we have endeavored to provide sane, logical, workable answers to these problems that so many of us have experienced at some time in our lives or, possibly, are experiencing at this very moment.

We sincerely ask you to read carefully, digest, and practice the important guidelines we give you, as they could well transform you *from the being you are into the very being you would like to be.*

Over the past decade there have been many books written on the subject of personal motivation, the majority of them excellent in their advice and application. The guidelines and advice that we offer are probably similar, but this has been written for the average, everyday person, with the emphasis on peace of mind and individuality as opposed to money or vast material gains. However, it is worth noting that the latter is invariably a by-product of achieving the former. So, if you are one of the many people who question the complexities and frustrations of life, then read on, for as you commence the next chapter, you may well be starting not only a new but the greatest chapter of your life.

The Answer Lies Within

When informing a person that his or her Numerological profile indicates writing ability, the answer is invariably, "I've often thought about writing, but how do I start?"

Before we begin to unravel some of life's mysteries, we must make a solemn pact between ourselves, a pact of honesty, because *nothing of benefit can be gleaned from these pages if you do not adhere to personal honesty.* Bearing this in mind, how would you now interpret the answer?

It is obvious the person has at least thought about the possibilities of writing, yet he or she has never explored the opportunities to put pen to paper. How do you start? Simply by buying a pen and writing pad, choosing a subject, and then writing.

The answer is so simple and free from complexities that we cannot reasonably assume that this solution has been overlooked by so many people. This leaves us with one alternative: that the person has considered it, but had not taken the thought further because he or she decided, "I can't write."

This same unenthusiastic approach also says, "I can't sing, I can't dance, I'm a failure." It is a sad fact that the majority of people have such a low opinion of themselves that failure is accepted and success never even considered.

Scientists have long known that habit is formed by repetition of a particular activity. If you light up a cigarette each time you talk on the telephone, it soon becomes a habit. If you always have your coffee break at 10:30 A.M., clean your shoes every second day, or even scratch your nose each time you have a problem, it very quickly becomes a subconscious, reflex action. The dictionary defines habit as a tendency to repeat an action in the same way: mental conditioning acquired by practice.

Unfortunately, the same logical conditioning applies to persons who continually say, "I can't," as very soon their mental computer programs the fact that they cannot fulfill the task in question. We all know that a computer can only act on the information or programs that are fed into it. Likewise, a computer can only relate true to that programming, as it does not possess reason.

Who can we then blame for this failure syndrome? The answer must be ourselves.

Through the ancient science of Numerology, we have endeavored to define your personality, your strengths, weaknesses, and potential in life. *Now we will set about the task of reprogramming your mental computer to work for you instead of against you.*

We have an exciting time ahead of us, as the results can often be dramatic. You will not have to wait months or years to see evidence of its worth, as step by step your life will quickly take on new dimensions, provided you believe in the concepts and work hard to make them succeed.

However, before you can be transformed, we must arm ourselves with some basic knowledge of life, for without it, your transformation will be short-lived and worthless in its effect.

The Laws of Life

THE FIRST LAW OF LIFE

Whatever your innermost mind can conceive your physical body can achieve.

Thought must precede action, for without thought there can be no action. This simply means that you can be what you conceive yourself to be. If you program yourself to conceive negatively, then you will be a negative person. But if you reprogram your computer to think positively and enthusiastically, then you will become a positive, enthusiastic individual.

No longer need you envy the successful and confident people you meet, because already you know one of the all-important secrets of their way of life. They are what they conceived themselves to be.

Think about this concept, savor its implications, and realize its strength.

We have discussed the "I can't" syndrome, realizing that it stems from our own negative programming. This we must blame on the *conscious* mind. Thankfully, however, each of us has a deeper level of mental activity, which we will refer to as our "innermost mind."

This deeper mental level is incapable of creating or activating thought processes that could be detrimental to our mental or physical well-being, as the greatest single force that lies within each and every one of us is self-preservation.

It is fortunate that our innermost mind will always consider what is totally best for us as a person, yet it is unfortunate that our conscious mind counteracts this singular individuality by creating confusion, loss of confidence and direction.

We can, therefore, assume that deep down each one of us is a positive individual, yet through circumstances, situations, and conditions we have developed a negative conscious side to our own personality that is our own worst enemy. This negative side is also frequently responsible for creating frustrations and resentments that can manifest themselves into psychosomatic illnesses and problems.

We all know the result that can be caused by two people constantly disagreeing—yet this is happening within us each and every day of our lives, often with the above result.

We can now define our mental ability to be ruled by the following two factors:

1. The innermost mind is always positive, as it reasons on a totally individual basis.
2. The conscious, self-programmed, negative mind frequently overrules the natural positive forces within us by creating confusion and loss of direction.

From these two assumptions we can make the following all-important conclusion:

As we program our conscious mind, we ourselves are to blame for the restrictions and limitations that it places on us.

Therefore, the first law of life can be achieved, provided the mental conscious level is prepared and willing to accept the challenge.

THE SECOND AND THIRD LAWS OF LIFE

Life's bountiful rewards are available to each and every one of us.

Before you exercise your conscious computer to say that the above law is impossible we will qualify this statement by including the third law of life, which says: *Your desire to achieve a goal in life must be so powerful that it overrules all other ambitions.*

To illustrate this point let's try a small exercise. Dust away the cobwebs of the past and go back to a time in your life when you really did want something. Can you remember how you desperately wanted or needed this particular thing in your life, and how you were prepared to give up anything to get it?

Even if you have a bad memory, this should be a relatively easy task, as successful accomplishments are always pleasant and therefore easier to remember.

Do you also remember how you amazed everybody—friends, relatives, and associates—when you actually did achieve your goal? Yet it did not surprise you. Why was this?

Your goal was reached because you had ruled out all possible doubt from your mind that it would not happen. From the point of thought conception you had achieved it and it had indeed happened within your mind already. You had overruled your conscious computer and reprogrammed it to concede to your desires and ultimate confidence. You had used your mind in the manner for which it was designed—*that of confident analysis and motivation.*

THE FOURTH LAW OF LIFE

Be yourself.

You are an individual unlike any other person on this earth. You have a right to individuality, a right to say what you think, and a right to act on what you believe is correct.

Most people reading this book are or have been involved in some occupation, profession, or trade. Before you could be proficient in your chosen field of endeavor, you had to learn about the many factors that went into making up the job. Success that you enjoyed or might have enjoyed came in direct proportion to the knowledge that you had gained in your subject.

It stands to reason that the best mechanics are those who have diligently studied their trade. Likewise, the most sought after advertising experts are men and women who have taken the time and trouble to learn their profession. Yet how many of us learn about ourselves?

Only our bodies and minds will be with us throughout our lives, from the second we are born to the second we depart from this earth. Doesn't it seem totally and utterly incomprehensible that we fail to take the time or effort to get to know ourselves? We learn about other people, our wives, husbands, children, friends, and associates, yet we overlook the most important factor of ourselves.

We are indeed like a ship without a rudder, wandering aimlessly through life without a thought or care for direction or guidance.

Before we can apply ourselves, we must be aware of ourselves, aware of all the finer points that go to make each and every one of us a complete individual. For without this knowledge, we cannot provide direction, and this factor is all-important to our happy and successful existence.

THE FIFTH LAW OF LIFE

Nothing of benefit can be derived from confusion.

Organization has won battles, launched rockets, planned massive empires and successful tea parties. It is essential to conceive a thought and to nullify all chance of failure, but we cannot overlook the importance of organization.

We have all, at some time in our lives, experienced the utter frustration of making decisions while in a confused state of mind. Yet the majority of us expect logical results from a disorganized existence.

This may seem the hardest law to abide by, yet in fact it is the easiest, as the next chapter will prove.

THE SIXTH LAW OF LIFE

The scales of life state that for effort given rewards must eventuate.

Most of us can remember back to our school days, when we were taught in chemistry that "Matter can neither be created nor destroyed in a chemical reaction." Effort is energy; therefore this same rule applies to life.

It is a simple fact that if you continue to put effort into a venture or occupation, eventually that effort will produce results. It may take weeks, months, or even years, but rest assured, sooner or later the sixth law of life will take control and success will be yours.

We can best illustrate this law by using an example. Consider life to be a set of scales. At one end we have a one ton weight which we will call our reward or eventual gain. On the other end of the scale, we have a one-pound weight which we will label "effort needed." At commencement, we place the pound weight on the scales, and as one would expect, nothing happens. The next day we place another pound of effort and still nothing happens. We continue to do this for a number of months, but still our effort does not produce results. Most of us at this time would tend to give up because we seem to be getting nowhere. But if we were to continue increasing our effort by the same proportion each day for a period of nearly six years, the scales would then begin to tip in our favor and the rewards we seek to gain would become ours.

Unfortunately this law cannot be defined any further, as effort required does not rule in direct proportion to the rewards sought. Often the impossible can be achieved in a very short space of time and the probable appears to take much longer. However, at present all we have to know and believe in is that this law of life does work.

THE SEVENTH LAW OF LIFE

Encourage and help others as they in turn will encourage and help you.

This law of life works on the same principle as the sixth law, that of equal reaction. Encouragement and help are actions that require effort; therefore they cannot be destroyed. By helping others, we are still loading the scales of life in favor of ourselves, so that our rewards can be realized sooner. Try wherever possible to help others. Criticize by all means, but endeavor to make your criticism constructive and not destructive, for remember the Bible also endorses this law by saying, "What you sow so shall you reap."

We need people, for few things, if any, can be achieved without the help of others.

Some people reading this law would say, "Impossible. How can one go through life helping others all the time? Charity begins at home." Or, "In business one can never do this."

If you are also having these same thoughts, think back through your life and try to remember one worthwhile thing that you did totally on your own without the help, encouragement, or consideration of others.

Remember, we are not applying these rules directly to money or material gains, but we are relating them to peace of mind, inner happiness, and fulfillment.

These seven important laws of life provide us with the necessary knowledge we need to set the wheels of reprogramming into action. We stated at the beginning of this chapter that without realization of these laws, success gained would be both short-lived and worthless in its effect. We now have the ammunition and knowledge needed to proceed, maintain success, and attract individuality and peace of mind.

However, before we take up the challenge of reprogramming, we must ask you to reason out the laws given in this chapter and make your own conclusions. If you agree with them, turn to the next chapter, but if you disagree, then at least set the wheels of effort into motion and give this book to a friend or associate who could make good use of it.

15

A New Beginning

An old saying in life is, "Everything comes to those who wait." However, experience has shown that while one person waits, another acts. We now believe that action is an effort and must produce results. So let's change that saying to, "Everything comes to those who act."

From this point on you must be prepared to act immediately on the steps given. Do not put them off to another day, as that day will never come. Act now and everything will indeed come to you. Your ladder of individuality awaits you, so let us take the first step.

The Five Important Steps

STEP 1

The fifth law of life taught us that nothing of benefit could be derived from confusion. Bearing this in mind we must now endeavor to turn the personal chaos of life into some semblance of order and priority. This is how we do it:

Sit down with a pen and writing pad and list all the jobs that must be completed by you personally to clear the chaotic cobwebs of your mind. Yes, put them all down, however small or petty they may be. Whether it is painting the house, getting the car insured, cleaning out the cupboards, getting the baby vaccinated, fixing the bathroom faucets —put them all down.

When you have completed your mental confusion checklist, check and recheck to make sure that nothing has been omitted. Now carefully number each entry in order of priority, making sure that you have listed them in their correct sequence. Now read this paragraph and then close the book, put it in a safe place, and forget about it. Now get cracking and complete all the jobs itemized on your mental confusion checklist —how can you organize your mind when you have so many physical liabilities confusing your everyday life?

One day—one week—one month later

You are back again. If you have followed this step honestly, you should be feeling one hundred percent better already. But if you are cheating and have not completed your mental confusion checklist, then you have nothing whatsoever to gain by reading further. So for your peace of mind, close the book and act.

STEP 2

Each and every one of us has problems. The more we think about them, the more insurmountable they become, until in the end the solution seems impossible. No longer will this be the case, as we are now going to act on these problems.

This time we will compile our problem list. Take a large sheet of paper and divide it into four columns, heading each column in the following manner from left to right: Column 1, Problem; Column 2, For; Column 3, Against; and Column 4, Solution.

Now list all the problems that are on your mind at present—yes, all of them, however petty they may be. As in step 1, number each of them in order of priority.

When you have completed and numbered this problem checklist, take each individual entry and reason out logically all the "fors" and "againsts," listing them in their respective columns. To illustrate this, let's look at a common, everyday problem.

Go through your complete checklist in this manner, itemizing the "fors" and "againsts" for each individual problem. Do not rush this exercise; take your time because it is essential that you include every possible "for" and "against" that could influence the problem in question.

As in step 1, read this next section and then put the book away.

There are many ways to complete a problem list, but the following has proven to be most successful:

1. Tackle only one problem at a time, in order of priority. Do not attempt to tackle a multitude of problems at the one time, as success will be greatly diminished.

Problem Checklist

Problem	For	Against	Solution
I have started a new job and I need another car, as my present vehicle is unreliable.	I can trade in my present vehicle. By purchasing a new car, I can expect twelve months of trouble-free travel. I can include my insurance in the finance repayments. I need a reliable vehicle, as my job depends on it. I am earning an extra $20 per week from my new position. The new registration on my present vehicle is due in one month.	I have not got enough money for the deposit and I am overcommitted on finance payments already. I still owe money on my present vehicle.	

2. Prior to going to sleep each night, read the first problem you have on your list. Absorb the "fors" and "againsts," but do not endeavor to solve the problem; just read all the alternatives open to you. Say to yourself while you are reading that you will have a trouble-free, peaceful night and that in the morning the solution will be clear and precise.
   We repeat: do not try to find the answer to the problem; just read the alternatives listed.
3. Put your list away in a safe place and go to sleep.
4. When you wake up in the morning, clear the sleep from your eyes and go immediately to your list. Read the alternatives again and then write down the first solution that comes into your mind.

5. *Act immediately on this solution* (we suggest you change from your pajamas or nightdress first).

6. When you have solved and acted on the problem in question, proceed to the next entry on your list and repeat the process. Do not move on to your next problem until the preceding one has been completely solved and acted on.

One day—one week—one month later

You are back again, and if you are not cheating, you should be feeling on top of the world, as your problems now rest securely in the past. Did you find that when you compiled your problem list it was shorter than you originally contemplated? This is common, as many small problems can be solved by one answer.

Life should start to take on a new meaning as you realize that the world is your oyster. However, we must crack open that oyster and see what is inside—by now you should be convinced that it is indeed a pearl.

STEP 3

Now that your mind is uncluttered with confusion and problems, we are going to recreate the successful you and highlight your true potential. When you studied your own Numerological profile earlier in this book, you would have reached various conclusions about yourself as an individual. The method shown below should provide further endorsement to these conclusions.

Sit down in a comfortable chair, away from the television, radio, and any other form of outside stimulus. Make sure that you will not be disturbed. Take the telephone off the hook and make sure that the baby is sound asleep. You will find this exercise is easier to complete if you are in a warm room. Take the now well-used pen and pad and place it on a table beside you. Spend the first ten minutes relaxing. Let the cares and worries (you should have very few by now anyway) just drift away. Mentally picture yourself relaxing in the sun on a secluded desert island, or sitting in a garden full of roses with the birds singing and the blue sky radiant above. It is unimportant what scene you mentally imagine as long as it does not involve physical activity. After a few attempts at this you will soon slip into a set pattern that is agreeable to your character.

When you feel completely and utterly relaxed, search back through your mind and try to remember situations or conditions that gave you complete happiness and a sense of fulfillment. Relive the events that

led up to this situation and enjoy again the wonderful feeling and satisfaction that it brought.

It might have been your first attempt at public speaking, when you
impressed twenty or so people with your gift for words. Possibly it was
the satisfaction of designing and making a new dress and wearing it to a
dance to be admired and commented on by so many people. Perhaps it
was the stimulating feeling of excitement as you won the finals of a
match, or even the satisfaction of helping someone in your community.

As these experiences pass through your mind, write down on your
pad what it was that you achieved, why you achieved it, and the feeling
you gained from achieving it. Repeat this process each day until you have
compiled your complete success and satisfaction list.

STEP 4

Now we want you to go through the same procedure as given in step 3,
but this time instead of listing your achievements, put down the failures
or distasteful events that occurred in your life. Relive the complete experience, writing down on your pad what caused these feelings and your
reactions at the time.

This list may take longer to compile than your previous success list,
as our minds tend to bury unpleasant experiences deep in the archives
of our brain. However, persist until you have listed and relived them one
by one.

By analyzing these two important lists, you should be able to tell at
a glance which subjects you excel or are happiest in and those that you
do not enjoy or are unsuitable to your individual character.

Remember this very important point: *It is so much easier to be
successful at a task you enjoy doing.*

So bearing this in mind, we can now completely rule out our failure
list and concentrate on our past successes and achievements. But before
we can turn the golden key to release our success mechanism, we must
move on to step 5.

STEP 5

Personality, situations, circumstances, and responsibilities. Obviously, situations arise that affect our very way of life. Some of them are totally
beyond our control, but many of them are self-induced.

We, the authors, have no desire or inclination to use this book as a platform to voice opinions relating to health or well-being of the body, except to bring to mind that we cannot abuse our bodies every day without having to pay in some way. Again the law of life comes into effect, as abuse is an action that in turn creates an opposite and equal reaction.

Any person can express the obvious opinion of eating the right foods, taking plenty of exercise and sleep, etc. But invariably, those quoting these utopian conditions are the people most guilty of bodily abuse themselves. We wholeheartedly agree that the above is important, but we offer the opinion that *self-abuse of the mind is far more detrimental than most other physical abuses of the body.*

If people live a life-style out of harmony or character with their true individuality, then their whole life-style will suffer as a direct consequence. By advising a person to stop eating the wrong foods, to take more exercise, or to stop smoking cigarettes, we are, in fact, treating the *result* rather than the *cause.*

Why do people smoke heavily, drink alcohol, take drugs, eat food to excess, or indulge in other vices? Simply because they need these crutches to help them face the realities of being locked into a life-style out of character with their very being. If you can lead a harmonious existence that offers personal fulfillment and satisfaction, these crutches would fall by the wayside since the body no longer needs them.

How does one treat or alter this personal dissatisfaction? Well, we are halfway there already, but we must now consider our individuality, responsibilities, circumstances, and situations that we find ourselves in.

This step is all important, as you must now realize more than ever that the life-style you desire to achieve must be both harmonious and compatible to the acceptable guidelines of your individual personality. This can simply be defined as, "There is no point in jumping out of the frying pan into the fire."

Consequently, we must define our true personality, liabilities, and responsibilities.

Arm yourself again with your trusty pen and paper and complete the following steps:

1. Define yourself honestly, accurately, and as precisely as you can. Try not to overlook any facets of your character. List the points you like and the points you dislike about yourself. But above all be completely honest in your appraisal.
2. List your responsibilities, liabilities, and financial obligations. This

may seem rather unnecessary, but believe us when we say that most people are totally unaware of their weekly financial commitments. So list your rent or mortgage payments, telephone, light and gas bills, food, insurance, finance commitments, and medical health payments. Calculate how much you spend at present on other items, such as entertainment, clothing, etc., and proportion this out to a weekly amount. When you have completed this list, check it to see that you have not overlooked any payments. Then add all the amounts together to arrive at one weekly figure. This now becomes your minimum livable amount. It is advisable not only to calculate one weekly livable figure, but to extend it to cover a further six- and twelve-month period. If you have young children, do not forget to include increased school fees, uniforms, etc. Also include a general ten percent, six-month increase to cover inflationary rises.

The reason why we suggest calculating minimum livable amounts for six and twelve months hence is because this will give you a firm, realistic guideline for the immediate future.

A business executive cannot be expected to make a decision without first being given the correct information so essential to his conclusions. Likewise, you cannot be expected to make decisions regarding yourself without first compiling information relating to your present position and circumstances.

If you have followed these steps carefully and honestly, you should now be in a position to make the all-important decisions based on the information you have gained. So to recap, you have:

1. Compiled and acted on your mental confusion checklist
2. Compiled and acted on your problem list
3. Compiled your success and satisfaction list
4. Compiled your failure and dissatisfaction list
5a. Compiled your individual personality assessment
5b. Compiled your financial liabilities and responsibilities list

Now you can stand up and take a bow, as already you have reached the select ten percent of the population; namely, those who have endeavored to define and organize their lives. From here on we are going to narrow down the percentages to enable you to reach the elite five percent category.

16

The Question Marks of Life

Read this chapter carefully, as the information you will gain from it should influence your decisions greatly.

ASK YOURSELF THE FOLLOWING QUESTIONS

Do you like yourself as a person?

When you completed your individual personality assessment, did the conclusions impress you?

If you met yourself at a party or social gathering, would you wish to know that person better and would or could you really become your own best friend?

It is reasonably logical to assume that if you are not impressed with your exterior manner, other people would not be impressed either.

Answer this important question. If you were to change your personality to become a much more likable person, would the changes be superficial and out of character, or would they be compatible with your true individuality?

Are you involved in life?

This may seem a somewhat unusual question, but it is based on a very real problem, as a great percentage of people are *not* involved in living. Through circumstances and because of certain situations, they have adopted a life-style of day-to-day existence rather than day-to-day involvement. Think about this statement, as there is a great deal of difference between the words "existence" and "involvement." Which category do you fall into?

Do you enjoy a meaningful relationship with people?

This is very similar to the previous question regarding involvement with living, as many people exist within a relationship that has ceased to become meaningful. This does not mean that the relationship should necessarily be terminated, but rather that it should be revitalized to renew or even increase the previously enjoyed meaningful companionship.

Would you like your children to share the same feelings and attitudes toward life that you do?

We are all aware of the tremendous personal responsibilities involved in raising children. Very few of us would knowingly impart incorrect knowledge or wisdom to our offspring. Yet, whether we like it or not, merely by living with us, they adopt similar attitudes to our own. Therefore, we could be responsible for their negative or pessimistic programming. Bearing this statement in mind we ask the question again:

Would you like your children to share the same feelings and attitudes toward life that you do?

If you could start all over again, would you still prefer to be the person you are now, living the same type of life-style?

Before you skip over this question, mentally saying it is impossible to turn back the clock, think about it, for although we cannot literally turn back the clock, we can still effect the same result.

Are you an enthusiastic person by nature? If not, why?

Again this question needs a great deal of thought, as it is extremely important for you to analyze why you are, have been, or have never been an enthusiastic individual. Try to remember what made you enthusiastic and, likewise, what dampened or eventually nullified your enthusiasm.

Are you pessimistic or optimistic by nature?

Similar to the previous question, try to determine why you are a pessimistic or optimistic person. Examine your past to see what created your optimism and likewise what was responsible for changing your optimistic attitude into one of pessimism. If you are and have always been a pessimistic person, try to define why you originally adopted this frame of mind.

Do you worry excessively?

Most of us spend a great deal of our lives worrying, usually over the minor, nonimportant problems of daily life. We inevitably cope under extreme emergencies, yet we enlarge these noneventful, minor problems into major complications. Try to remember why you worried so much over a particular problem, think back to see if it did, in fact, either alter the situation or provide the answer. Examine what is worrying you now. Do you consider yourself to be a born worrier? If so, why?

Can you accept the inevitable?

When major problems or circumstances have occurred, have you accepted the outcome or the limitations that were placed on you as a direct result, or have you spent the time since contemplating what life would have been like if the circumstances had, in fact, never happened?

Are you a determined person?

Some of us are naturally determined individuals who will fight with every ounce of energy to pursue goals and ambitions in life, yet others are easily discouraged. Which category do you fit into? If you are not a determined person, analyze why you give in so easily. Look at your past and endeavor to find the cause for this lack of determination. Think carefully, as the answer will be there.

Do you envy other people?

Examine carefully what it is you envy about other people. Forget about money or material affluence; instead, concentrate on their attitude toward life, their physical bearing, manner, and character. Try to establish whether these qualities would be acceptable to your own personality. Mentally switch places with them. Would you really prefer to be them instead of yourself?

Do other people admire you?

This is a reverse of the above question. Try to analyze what it is about your character or personality that appeals to other people. Reconstruct past situations where people have shown their admiration for you and determine why they admired you.

If you have been completely honest with yourself while answering these questions, you should now have a wealth of valuable information at your fingertips: information about you, the person as you are and as others see you. Some of the points you have discovered have probably shocked you with their implications; others have possibly surprised you with their simplicity. But above all, you are now aware of them.

17

The Four Steps to Freedom

Your reprogramming is now almost complete, except for one final, very important exercise. If you were to stop here, the information gained so far would prove to be invaluable to your everyday private and business life. However, there does remain the last important step, *a step that does indeed provide the golden key to inner happiness and individuality.*

The method given below is simple but very effective. We sincerely ask you at least to give it a try so that you can judge the results for yourself.

This is a gradual exercise that must not be forced or rushed and should be completed over a period of approximately four to five weeks, with a minimum of one session per night of at least thirty minutes' duration.

STEP 1

Retire each night at the same time to a warm room. Position yourself in a comfortable chair and just relax. As with the success and failure checklist exercise, imagine yourself relaxing in some faraway desert island without a care in the world. If you have been following the other exercises carefully, you should have by now developed your own relaxing pattern.

Spend the first ten minutes just letting the tension slip away; feel the warm sensation of muscles relaxing and your body recharging itself.

Now we ask you to remember back to your personality character appraisal and to the questions in the previous chapter. Reconstruct, piece by piece, the person you would most like to be. Be very realistic about this reconstruction, bearing in mind all the factors we have discussed regarding compatibility and harmonious existence.

Do not try to reconstruct a person that would be totally out of character with your very being.

For your first and second session just adhere to the above, carefully formulating the person you would dearly love to be. If you know one of your faults is talking too much, then imagine yourself listening and only talking when you have something important and worthwhile to say. If you are an introverted person who is uncomfortable in the company of others, reconstruct a person who is confident—not too confident; just more so than you are at present.

Do not try to construct a perfect person—be totally *realistic*.

Do not proceed with the second step until you have formulated your ideal person, a person who would be totally compatible to your very nature and character.

STEP 2

Go through your normal ten-minute relaxing period and when you are completely calm and serene, imagine the person you have reconstructed and spend about five minutes just familiarizing yourself with this individual.

Now relive most or all of the events that took place in your life today, but substitute the new you for the old you. Now imagine how the new you would react to situations that occurred, as opposed to your own reactions that actually took place. Try to establish in your mind how the new you would, in fact, have lived the day under the same conditions.

If this new you appeals to your very individuality and the results of this exercise are pleasing, then repeat this step for a period of three to four individual sessions, each time examining and reliving the previous twelve hours of your life.

If the new you does not appeal to your character, then stop the exercise immediately and revert back to step 1 and remold this individual, based on the experience you have gained so far.

STEP 3

Again spend ten minutes relaxing and a further five minutes familiarizing yourself with the new you.

This time, instead of reliving the previous twelve hours, go back in your life to major events that occurred and relive these experiences, substituting the new you for the old you.

Compare how this person handled the situations. See how the new you dealt with your successful accomplishments and also see how he or she fared when dealing with your previous failures. If you are impressed with the result, then move on to step 4. But if you are unsatisfied, go back to the beginning and from your experience, remold and streamline the new you.

STEP 4

As with each of the other three steps, spend the first ten minutes relaxing and the next five minutes familiarizing yourself with the new you.

This time you are going to consider tomorrow—the next day in your life. You should have a good idea of what tomorrow holds for you. Whether it is a day of home chores and shopping or a day of business and appointments. Make your new identity live this next day of your life.

Try to anticipate situations that will probably occur and likewise see how he or she handles them. Repeat this step of the exercise each night for a period of at least three weeks.

18
The Real You

Welcome back.

The new you has become the real you. How does it feel? Does it feel right? Do you look forward to getting up in the morning? Are your relationships with people improving? Is life taking on a new meaning? Your answer should be yes to all of these questions

Your reprogramming finishes here because the real you should now be suitably equipped to realize and put into action all of the points discussed in this part of the book.

Opportunities that rarely occurred in the past will now happen every day, as your true self will be automatically guided in the right direction. The forces of life are now working *for* you instead of *against* you.

In parting, we ask you to reread the laws of life, which should now mean much more to you than they ever did before. Endeavor to practice each one of them, as they are indeed so valuable to your continued success.

If this book has helped you, then it has achieved its task.

May you enjoy and live each day of your life to the full.

For your convenience, the following blank Key Word Preparation Charts have been included to enable you to compile your own Natal chart resume, or those of your friends and family.

Key Word Preparation Chart

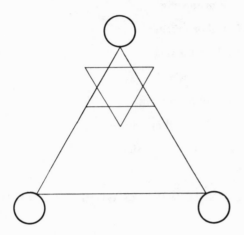

Name _____

Date of Birth: Month ☐   Day ☐   Year ☐

       Life Path Number = ☐

ASPECTS SHOWN WITHIN THE NATAL CHART

(1) Number of digits ☐

(2) Number of digits ☐

(3) Number of digits ☐

(4) Number of digits ☐

(5) Number of digits ☐

(6) Number of digits ☐

(7) Number of digits ☐

(8) Number of digits ☐

(9) Number of digits ☐

FULL AND MISSING LINES WITHIN THE NATAL CHART

Thought line (1–2–3) full or missing

Will line (4–5–6) full or missing

Action line (7–8–9) full or missing

Mind line (3–6–9) full or missing

Soul line (2–5–8) full or missing

Physical line (1–4–7) full or missing

Determination line (1–5–9) full or missing

Compassion line (3–5–7) full or missing

MISSING SINGLE NUMBERS WITHIN THE NATAL CHART

(1)

(2)

(3)

(4)

(5)

(6)

(7)

(8)

(9)

LIFE PATH NUMBER CHARACTERISTICS

Positive

Negative

Average

Home, marriage, and partners

Suitable occupations

DAY NUMBER CHARACTERISTICS

Key Word Preparation Chart

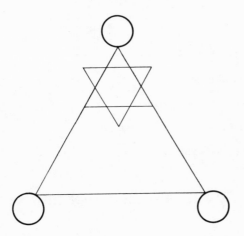

Name _____

Date of Birth: Month ☐ Day ☐ Year ☐

  Life Path Number = ☐

ASPECTS SHOWN WITHIN THE NATAL CHART

(1) Number of digits ☐

(2) Number of digits ☐

(3) Number of digits ☐

(4) Number of digits ☐

(5) Number of digits ☐

(6) Number of digits ☐

(7) Number of digits ☐

(8) Number of digits ☐

(9) Number of digits ☐

FULL AND MISSING LINES WITHIN THE NATAL CHART

Thought line (1–2–3) full or missing

Will line (4–5–6) full or missing

Action line (7–8–9) full or missing

Mind line (3–6–9) full or missing

Soul line (2–5–8) full or missing

Physical line (1–4–7) full or missing

Determination line (1–5–9) full or missing

Compassion line (3–5–7) full or missing

MISSING SINGLE NUMBERS WITHIN THE NATAL CHART

(1)

(2)

(3)

(4)

(5)

(6)

(7)

(8)

(9)

LIFE PATH NUMBER CHARACTERISTICS

Positive

Negative

Average

Home, marriage, and partners

Suitable occupations

DAY NUMBER CHARACTERISTICS